Palgrave Studies in Science and Popular Culture

Series Editor
Sherryl Vint, Department of English, University of California, Riverside,
USA

This book series seeks to publish ground-breaking research exploring the productive intersection of science and the cultural imagination. Science is at the centre of daily experience in twenty-first century life and this has defined moments of intense technological change, such as the Space Race of the 1950s and our very own era of synthetic biology. Conceived in dialogue with the field of Science and Technology Studies (STS), this series will carve out a larger place for the contribution of humanities to these fields. The practice of science is shaped by the cultural context in which it occurs and cultural differences are now key to understanding the ways that scientific practice is enmeshed in global issues of equity and social justice. We seek proposals dealing with any aspect of science in popular culture in any genre. We understand popular culture as both a textual and material practice, and thus welcome manuscripts dealing with representations of science in popular culture and those addressing the role of the cultural imagination in material encounters with science. How science is imagined and what meanings are attached to these imaginaries will be the major focus of this series. We encourage proposals from a wide range of historical and cultural perspectives.

Advisory Board:
Mark Bould, University of the West of England, UK
Lisa Cartwright, University of California, US
Oron Catts, University of Western Australia, Australia
Melinda Cooper, University of Sydney, Australia
Ursula Heise, University of California Los Angeles, US
David Kirby, University of Manchester, UK
Roger Luckhurt, Birkbeck College, University of London, UK
Colin Milburn, University of California, US
Susan Squier, Pennsylvania State University, US

Karina Judd · Bridget Gaul ·
Anna-Sophie Jürgens

Women Scientists in American Television Comedy

Beakers, Big Bangs and Broken Hearts

Karina Judd 🆔
The Australian National University
Canberra, ACT, Australia

Bridget Gaul 🆔
The Australian National University
Canberra, ACT, Australia

Anna-Sophie Jürgens 🆔
The Australian National University
Canberra, ACT, Australia

ISSN 2731-4359   ISSN 2731-4367   (electronic)
Palgrave Studies in Science and Popular Culture
ISBN 978-3-031-81524-9   ISBN 978-3-031-81525-6   (eBook)
https://doi.org/10.1007/978-3-031-81525-6

CONTENTS

About the Authors

Karina Judd is a PhD graduate of The Australian National Centre for the Public Awareness of Science at The Australian National University (ANU) in Canberra, Australia. Her doctoral research was on inclusive science communication research and practice around the world; building on her past professional experiences as a science communicator, science outreach facilitator, environmental geologist and geoarchaeologist. Karina has been a tutor and mentor for students within the Popsicule, ANU's Science in Pop Culture and Entertainment Hub.

Bridget Gaul is a postgraduate medical student at The Australian National University School of Medicine and Psychology. Her research interests include the representations of gender, cultural and occupational groups in different media forms, particularly within STEM contexts and science and humor.

Anna-Sophie Jürgens is a senior lecturer in Science Communication at The Australian National Centre for the Public Awareness of Science at The Australian National University (ANU) and the head of the Popsicule, ANU's Science in Pop Culture and Entertainment Hub. Her research explores the cultural meanings of science, the history of (violent) clowns and mad scientists, science and humor, and the interface between science and (public) art.

LIST OF TABLES

CHAPTER 1

"Even Female Scientists Can Land a Man": Introduction

Abstract This chapter introduces the book *Women Scientists in American Television Comedy: Beakers, Big Bangs and Broken Hearts*, focusing on the representation of women scientists in popular media and the role of humor in shaping cultural perceptions of science. The chapter emphasizes how popular culture, including comedy shows, influences public attitudes toward science by constructing perceptions of scientists. Despite the increasing presence of women in STEM, their representation in media remains limited and stereotyped, often conforming to traditional gender roles. The chapter explores how humor and comedy have historically been male-dominated, with women marginalized in the production and consumption of public humor. It also discusses the "Matilda Effect", where women's scientific achievements are often ignored or miscredited to men. The chapter sets the stage for the book's analysis of how TV comedies portray women scientists, focusing on series like *Never Have I Ever*, *The Big Bang Theory* and *Zoey's Extraordinary Playlist*. It outlines the research questions and methodologies used to examine the humor types characterizing these portrayals and their impact on cultural ideas of women in STEM. The chapter highlights the importance of understanding humor's role in communicating science and shaping public perceptions of women scientists.

Keywords Cultural meanings of science · Science in pop culture · Humor and science · Representations of scientists · Gender and science · Women in STEM

Popular culture and entertainment are versatile frames for interpreting our relationship with scientific discourses. Science-related cultural products—including comedy shows and television programs—are vehicles of science communication as they reflect ideas about science and "construct perceptions for both the public and scientists in a mutual shaping of science and culture" (Kirby, 2008, p. 44). Studies of science popularization demonstrate that "its cultural meanings, and not its knowledge, may be the most significant element contributing to public attitudes toward science" and that "[p]opular images of science can significantly influence public attitudes toward it by shaping, cultivating, or reinforcing these 'cultural meanings' of science" (Kirby, 2017, p. 11; cf. Flicker 2008). Cultural meanings and popular images of science are created and propagated in popular entertainment and media. Science in film and television can therefore prompt us to "move beyond simplistic notions of science" as a mere collection of facts in a textbook and "to consider science as a larger cultural institution" (Davies et al., 2019, p. 8). Within this context, however, there has been little discussion of the role of humor and comic performance in shaping, if not defining, the cultural representation—or cultural meanings—of the scientist character, although interest in the use of humor in and for communicating science and in science comedy has gained momentum in recent years (e.g. Boykoff & Osnes, 2019; Cacciatore et al., 2020; Kaltenbacher & Drews, 2020; Pinto et al., 2015; Simis-Wilkinson et al., 2018; Soucy-Humphreys et al., 2023). This is surprising because humor and comic performance are powerful tools in communication. Indeed, whether as a fictional genre or as a form of entertainment, comedy is a compelling cultural and social phenomenon that influences and connects people, knowledge, understanding and information (Boykoff & Osnes, 2019, p. 154). Comedy can serve as impactful social commentary, speak truth to power, push boundaries and provide relief from the absurdities of human existence. With its multifaceted and even paradoxical function, humor in comedy can transgress and reverse hegemonic stereotypes, challenge hierarchies and divisions, but also reinforce, deepen, dramatize and extend these same social ideologies

(McIntosh, 2014, p. 42; Lockyer, 2020, p. 3; Riquelme et al., 2023). It is thus not surprising that comedians are called "cultural mediators and public sociologists" (Cooper, 2019, p. 92).

Historically, comic performance has been the privilege of men (cf. Lockyer, 2011, pp. 114–115 on the stand-up comedyscape; Dickinson et al., 2014; Lockyer, 2020, p. 2). Comedy is no stranger to patriarchal limitations, as historically women have been marginalized in the production and consumption of public humor, whereas men were believed to have superior humorous expression (Johnston, 2014, p. 53; Kuipers, 2006). Research into the history and performance traditions of lady clowns, for example, shows that comic women-impersonators and (male) ballet parodists in tutus, as well as women playing male comic performers, have shaped 'female' clown performances on popular stages for centuries, before female clowning began to challenge the masculinist discourse of earlier forms of clowning only a few decades ago (Jürgens, 2021), acting as a catalyst for new performance aesthetics. As Dickinson et al. show in their 2014 book *Women and Comedy: History, Theory, Practice,* earlier theorists of comedy (such as Freud and Bergson) saw women neither as agents nor spectators of comedy, but only as its targets. Only recently has the scholarly study of comedy begun to acknowledge and historicize both the lack of comic female role models in comic (popular) theater and women's contributions to comedy, with intersectional examinations of these contributions increasing in the last few years.

As a result of similar patriarchal cultural forces, there are striking similarities in the portrayal of comic characters and scientists in popular media: the latter has tended to be dominated by privileged white men, with women barely represented (Kirby, 2017). This narrow portrayal in media of "pale, stale, male" scientists (Lawler, 1996, p. 800) is emblematic of what Margaret Rossiter (1993) called the "Matilda Effect", where the scientific achievements of women have been ignored, downplayed or miscredited to male colleagues or partners—even non-existent men. In the real-life STEM workplace, the Matilda Effect has been shown to influence women's recognition in the sciences from history to today, including women's underrepresentation in professional awards (Lincoln et al., 2012), academic publication writing and reviewing opportunities (Helmer et al., 2017; Knobloch-Westerwick et al., 2013) and conference presentations (Jones et al., 2014). Against this background, the discussion of scientist stereotypes—women stereotypes in particular—has diversified considerably, notably in moving away from analyses of 'clear-cut types' (in the 'tradition' of Gorp et al., 2014; Haynes, 2003, 2016), thus exploring more complex and nuanced facets of cultural portrayals of scientists (see, e.g., Kirby, 2017; Locke, 2005; Willey & Subramaniam, 2017). Very few recent publications, however, examine the role of humor within this context, humorous depictions of (women) scientists in entertainment or the link between comic performance and science (exceptions include, e.g. Jones, 1997; Soucy-Humphreys et al., 2023; Terzian & Grunzke, 2007). In other words, while it has been recognized that the image of scientists in culture "must be understood as a surprisingly stable combination of persistent stereotypes and changing patterns" (Hüppauf & Weingart, 2007, p. 5), there is a dearth of research addressing questions about comic representations of women scientists, despite a growing interest in humorous public science events, science stand-up routines, science comedy and even science-based sitcoms (e.g. Bankes, 2023; Riesch, 2015).

Like Billig (2005, p. 214) and Jontes and Trdina before us (2018, p. 52), we argue that the seriousness of the social world—including the realm of science as a cultural institution—is intrinsically linked to comedy. We also agree that "[e]mphasizing the role of humor is important because television comedies are commonly described in public discourse as just for fun" (Jontes & Trdina, 2018, p. 52)—which is worth a closer look and, indeed, reconsideration. Using the term "woman scientist" to refer to anyone identifying as a woman working in science (a term previously used by Flicker, 2008), technology, engineering or mathematics, we pose the following research question: **What types of humor characterize portrayals of women scientists in mainstream American comedy television and how is this humor used to shape cultural ideas of (the reality of) women in STEM?** Focusing on the TV series *Never Have I Ever*, *The Big Bang Theory* and *Zoey's Extraordinary Playlist*, we will examine in the following what kind of humor these women scientists use to communicate science, how these comedic TV portrayals of women scientists reflect the lived experience of women scientists and what their comic performances contribute to our understanding of cultural ideas and public images of science.

ABOUT THIS BOOK

Women Scientists in American Television Comedy: Beakers, Big Bangs and Broken Hearts consists of six chapters that analyze and interpret the relationship between "what is shown and what can be perceived as real" in selected episodes of science-related TV series as sites of humor-related "cultural circulation" (Flicker, 2008, p. 243)—where diverse discourses, aesthetic practices and humor strategies, and the worlds of imagined scientists interact; in combination with stereotypes that reveal the importance of cultural contexts for STEM fields. Informed by previous research on women stereotypes in science and pop culture, science communication and humor theory, we examine a total of 47 episodes of three popular TV comedies through textual analysis to better understand how their women scientist protagonists were portrayed through humor, and how their portrayal reinforced or challenged gender conventions in these fictional representations of the scientific profession and (the reality of) science.

To set the scene, Chapter 2 offers an extensive overview of existing research and discourses around the key themes of 'real' and fictional experiences of women scientists. The chapter contains the following six sub-sections:

Underrepresentation of Women in STEM: Women have historically been excluded from STEM as both an interest and a career, with this exclusion continuing through to today. Exclusion has arisen from many diverse factors, with both obvious and subtle impacts that reverberate through the profession today. What would a snapshot through statistics of uptake of STEM careers by women uncover? We explore the context behind the existing gender gaps with an overview of barriers and their impacts, showing the need for research examining the varied ways that women are introduced to, inspired by and develop a sense of belonging in STEM careers.

Stereotyping of Women in STEM and *Underrepresentation of Women Scientists in Media*: Past research has revealed that the way in which women in STEM are perceived and portrayed often conforms to a number of stereotypes that do not necessarily reflect the realities of being a woman in STEM today. What do we know about these stereotypes—where do they come from, how do they manifest—and how do they undermine both women and STEM as a whole? Compared to their male counterparts, women scientists are portrayed less frequently in the media, reflecting cultural biases and stereotypes of STEM as a 'masculine' pursuit. As shown in these sections with powerful clarity, the balance of both fictional and non-fictional representations are skewed against women scientists in the media.

Ideologies of Gender and STEM in Media: Media representations of scientists have been shown to lack diversity in general, and certainly so when investigated with a gender lens. Examining the research précised above uncovered that traditional (Western) gender roles, gender stereotypes and STEM stereotypes result in a narrowing of the way that women in STEM are portrayed in the media, which emphasized femininity, beauty, motherhood and domestic roles. We endeavor to explore the implications of these stereotype-entrenched portrayals, given the context that, for many people in the population who have limited interaction with STEM spaces, these will be core influences in their understanding of STEM. This means that normalizing negative stereotypes within these media portrayals can filter into negative beliefs about the 'type of person' who belongs in STEM—whether that is defined by gender, values, personality or other characteristics. Conversely, positive—and indeed, humorous—representations of people in STEM fields can lead to positive associations with STEM, and has been shown to influence STEM as a desirable field of study and work through media representations acting as positive role models. In this subsection we provide a rationale as to why such representations are important, with its ability to influence identity, perceptions and behaviors of audiences.

Women and Humor: Comic performance, like science, has historically been viewed as a masculine domain, with women's participation marginalized and their comedic voices often silenced. However, this stereotype is changing as both historical and contemporary roles of women in comedy are being recognized, highlighting their contributions to feminist advancement and their use of comedy to explore and subvert social taboos. This sub-section contrasts sexist humor—and its harmful effects on both individuals and society—with subversive, feminist humor. Then we briefly explore arguments by feminist scholars that increased opportunities for women in comedy are essential to reversing social myths, and allowing marginalized voices to speak truth to power, express identities and convey joy.

Humor, the Communication of Science and Comedic Portrayals of Women STEM Professionals in TV: Explanations of what humor is are as varied as the theories of humor. Focusing on key theories and definitions, we turn specifically to the role of humor in Science Communication, noting that this area has been explored previously in the context of *The Big Bang Theory*. However, we identify that to date there has been little analysis focused on the women scientist in particular. We demonstrate that this book addresses this gap, going further by comparing and contrasting the representations of women scientists in more recent television shows, *Never Have I Ever* and *Zoey's Extraordinary Playlist*. Our approach to these TV series follows Eva Flicker's (2008) understanding of stereotypes and mass media's involvement in constructing depictions of social reality that ultimately contribute to the public's understanding of science and scientists.

Chapter 3 introduces the rationale of the research presented hereafter—the central interpretive frameworks, sample strategy and analytical process. Our study draws on three interpretive frameworks—two around the stereotypes of fictional women scientists, and one typology of humor. Flicker (2008) developed a seminal model of the seven archetypes of women scientist stereotypes, which we combine with the primary themes of women scientist characters identified by Steinke (2005). Adopting a combination of these interpretive contexts, we aim to understand if, and what, humor is used in scenes portraying women scientists and how this portrayal contributes to and is shaped by cultural ideas of women in STEM. For our investigation of the specific humor in comedic television portrayals of women scientists, we draw from and expand on a humor typology published in 2004 by Moniek Buijzen and Patti M. Valkenburg, which brings together many of the humor theories mentioned above. Buijzen and Valkenburg take into account different humor theories in the development of their typology, and show that many humor types are not necessarily funny—"they must complement one another to generate humor" (Buijzen & Valkenburg, 2004, p. 149).

The three series, from which episodes were selected to form our corpus and focus of our qualitative analysis, are popular and internationally successful television series. They are part of the contemporary media culture in the United States from which they originate, but as American media culture is increasingly present throughout the world, we follow Douglas Kellner in considering them of "global and not merely regional interest" (2020, p. 9). This part of the book thus provides a perspective on the usefulness of Humanities research methods in a Science Communication research context, an approach that is much less common in this space than qualitative methodologies drawn from the Social Sciences.

We hope that this study will act as a reference point for this type of investigation in a field that is proud of its trans- and inter-disciplinary nature.

In Chapter 4 we present our findings in light of five key questions and how these, together, respond to our research question:

1. How is humor used when portraying the expertise and competence of women scientists?
2. How is humor used when portraying the working relationship between male colleagues and women scientists?
3. How is humor used when portraying the work-life balance of women scientists?
4. How is humor used in the portrayal of women scientist stereotypes?
5. How is humor used in the portrayal of traditional gender stereotypes of women?

Questions 1–3 focus on science as occupation, while Questions 4–5 concentrate on stereotypes of women in STEM. We find some overlap of these categories, however, with humor techniques like irony, for example, being commonly used in relation to women's expertise in the way that they are forced to struggle for acknowledgment alongside their male colleagues' lesser achievements. This chapter draws heavily on direct quotes and specific scenes from episodes in all three series studied to illustrate the humor techniques deployed and how, in context, they draw attention to the ways that the female characters negotiate their STEM experiences—both positive and negative.

Chapter 5 unpacks that the most common humor types used in relation to the women scientist characters overall were irony and satire. According to Buijzen and Valkenburg's (2004) humor typology, these humor types echo one specific humor theory (the Superiority Theory), as they involve outwitting others and laughing at the misfortunes of others. Also drawn from their investigation, we discover that satire and irony, being more complex humor categories, appeal more to a general and adolescent audience, likely due to these age groups having a greater appreciation for more sophisticated forms of humor compared to children (Acuff & Reiher, 1997), while also appealing to the non-compliant attitude of adolescents (Buijzen & Valkenburg, 2004). When comparing humor aimed at different gender groups, adult women tended to appreciate nonsensical and silly humor, like that of slapstick, compared to the more malicious preferences of men (Buijzen & Valkenburg, 2004, p. 152). This finding is consistent with previous studies of humor preferences, which suggest men prefer more caustic and disparaging humor (e.g. irony and satire), while women prefer innocent humor categories (e.g. clownish humor and surprise, Brodzinsky et al., 1981; Johnson, 1992). This is interesting, as while our study found that the women scientist characters serve as both the humorous subject and vehicle to humorously ridicule others (frequently male characters or patriarchal structures), according to Buijzen and Valkenburg (2004) this humor may not be directed for a female audience. However, our findings also highlight that scenes that use the humor types of irony, satire, ridicule and schadenfreude typically criticize male characters and portray the women scientist as intellectually and socially superior, suggesting a subversive, feminist underpinning. But ultimately, this humor is rooted in a complex interplay of feminist and sexist perspectives. We explain this in more detail in Chapter 5, which also includes a close reading of the women scientist characters, making sense of their portrayals within a comic frame.

Affirming the "increasingly prevalent sense that science communication is not external to (popular) culture" (Davies et al., 2019, p. 2), our study found—as the conclusion in Chapter 6 shows—that a wide range of humor types was used in the portrayal of different aspects of women scientists' life experiences. The most common types of humor were irony and satire, with much of the humor based on an awareness of existing gender stereotypes. The humorous use of irony often hides anti-feminist discourse through the use of ironic sexism. However, in line with feminist approaches to and understandings of humor, ironic humor is also frequently used to ridicule male characters and criticize patriarchal structures in STEM arenas. Marginalized groups can use humor strategically to challenge powerlessness. In this way, subversive humor—including satire or parody—leading to the creation of alternative scripts "within the parameters of the prevailing social order, ultimately to critique it", has been called "a form of micro-revolution" (Longo, 2010, p. 123). Uncovering the utility of humor for women scientist characters adds a new dimension to Petra Pansegrau's idea that media not only communicates scientific information but contributes to scientific discourse in public domains through its construction and depiction of knowledge (Pansegrau, 2008, p. 257). Thus, our study shows TV comedies play a crucial role in this process by contributing "to science's construction of meaning" (Flicker, 2008, p. 242). In conjunction with complex women scientists' representations that move beyond the characteristics identified by Flicker (2008), feminist humor in TV comedies is a powerful tool to reform preconceptions of STEM and empower young women to pursue STEM. Our research conclusion highlights both the versatility of humor and its power to reflect, reinforce and move beyond traditional gender stereotypes. Far from being the target of jokes in popular entertainment, science is a driver of performance style and contributes to the creation of comic forms. Within this context, comic representations of women scientists participate in and contribute to complex cultural inquiry and transmedial public discourses—and, ultimately, the cultural power and cultural work of science.

This book explores the representations of the convergence of cisgender womanhood and STEM as a career in the early twenty-first century through American TV comedy. The book refers to ideas of woman-hood and femininity within a culture that often places these in binary opposition to manhood and masculinity (Hyde et al., 2019). However, activists and academics have increasingly differentiated between sex and the lived experience of gender (see, e.g., Acker (1992) for a relatively early perspective on this shift; see Hyde et al. (2019) for a more recent review), including applying these with the context of scientific research (e.g. Rioux et al., 2022; Subramaniapillai et al., 2024). Yet representa-tions of gender-diverse characters are relatively scarce on television, and when present have often been negative and lacking nuance (Capuzza & Spencer, 2016; O'Meara & Monaghan, 2024). There are signs that this is changing, however, with increasing representation of complex gender identities among television characters (e.g. O'Meara & Monaghan, 2024; Villegas Simón et al., 2023). The TV series that form the basis of this book do not feature explicitly transgender or non-binary scientist char-acters, so most instances of 'woman', 'female' , and similar phrases refer to cisgender women throughout, reflecting the language used within the shows.

WHY STUDY THE HUMOR OF BEAKERS, BIG BANGS AND BROKEN HEARTS?

By exploring the cultural meanings of science, we aim to better under-stand how pop cultural narratives about science have affected the public discourse and understanding of science, and thus the science-society relationship. Popular media, including television shows, and audience identification with their protagonists have been studied as a source of audience influence and as variables that can affect perceptions of norms, if not behavioral norms and changes (see, e.g., Rhodes & Ellithorpe, 2016, p. 362). Given that women have historically been sidelined in both TV comedies and TV portrayals of science, a better understanding of their representation and dynamics in contemporary popular entertainment can be influential in the interests of young women's engagement in STEM (cf. Geena Davis Institute on Gender in Media, 2018; Steinke, 2012). By reflecting or interpreting the dominant social values of society, media representations of women associated with STEM spaces—including representations of comic women scientists—have the power to directly influence the uptake of such careers by young women (Chimba & Kitzinger, 2010; Fogg-Rogers & Hobbs, 2019; Steinke, 1999, 2012).

This book is committed to diversifying our understanding of science in culture: Exploring portrayals of science beyond the ubiquitous pop cultural master narrative of mad scientists, horror-technology running amok and Frankensteinian violent delights, the following pages reconsider stereotypical depictions of science—and shed new light on the cultural power of science through humor. This can add new dimensions to the richness and multidimensionality of the cultural capital of science. By discovering narratives that illuminate the multiple interactions of science with humor and comedy, this book offers a deeper account of our cultural imagination of science than has been previously established, while also spotlighting how the field of pop culture has been integrated into our contemporary perceptions of science. Within this context, TV comedies featuring scientists provide enjoyment and other affective responses (such as amusement) to the science themes at stake and thus may form, reform or confirm science-related opinions (Burns et al., 2003, p. 190). Or, in other words and from a much broader perspective, comedic approaches and humor can "influence how meanings course through the veins of our social body" (Boykoff & Osnes, 2019). Examining how women scientists are "incorporated into the common culture" (Bryant, 2003, p. 357) through humor, this book contributes to the study of both, the intangible cultural aspects of and in Science Communication (cf. Davies et al., 2019) and the role of humor in communicating science themes and meanings.

REFERENCES

Acuff, D. S., & Reiher, R. H. (1997). *What kids buy and why*. Free Press.

Acker, J. (1992). From sex roles to gendered institutions. *Contemporary Sociology, 21*(5), 565–569. https://doi.org/10.2307/2075528

Bankes, E. T. (2023). Laughing to love science: Contextualizing science comedy. *Humor, 36*(1), 75–94. https://doi.org/10.1515/humor-2022-0030

Billig, M. (2005). *Laughter and ridicule: Towards a social critic of humour*. Sage.

Boykoff, M., & Osnes, B. (2019). A laughing matter? Confronting climate change through humor. *Political Geography, 68*, 154–163. https://doi.org/10.1016/j.polgeo.2018.09.006

Brodzinsky, D. M., Barnet, K., & Aiello, J. R. (1981). Sex of subject and gender identity as factors in humor appreciation. *Sex Roles, 7*, 561–573.

Bryant, C. (2003). Does Australia need a more effective policy of science communication? *International Journal for Parasitology, 4*(33), 357–361. https://doi.org/10.1016/s0020-7519(03)00004-3

Buijzen, M., & Valkenburg, P. M. (2004). Developing a typology of humor in audiovisual media. *Media Psychology, 6*(2), 147–167. https://doi.org/10.1207/s1532785xmep0602_2

Burns, T. W., O'Connor, D. J., & Stocklmayer, S. M. (2003). Science communication: A contemporary definition. *Public Understanding of Science, 12*, 183–202. https://doi.org/10.1177/09636625030122004

Cacciatore, M A., Becker, A. B., Anderson, A. A., & Yeo, S. K. (2020). Laughing with science. The influence of audience approval on engagement. *Science Communication, 42*(2), 195–217. https://doi.org/10.1177/1075547020910749.

Capuzza, J. C., & Spencer, L. G. (2017). Regressing, progressing, or transgressing on the small screen? Transgender characters on U.S. scripted television series. *Communication Quarterly, 65*(2), 214–230. https://doi.org/10.1080/01463373.2016.1221438

Chimba, M., & Kitzinger, J. (2010). Bimbo or Boffin? Women in science: An analysis of media representations and how female scientists negotiate cultural contradictions. *Public Understanding of Science, 19*(5), 609–624. https://doi.org/10.1177/0963662510377233

Cooper, K. S. (2019). What's so funny? Audiences of women's stand-up comedy and layered referential viewing: Exploring identity and power. *The Communication Review, 22*(2), 91–116. https://doi.org/10.1080/10714421.2019.1599666

Davies, S. R., Halpern, M., Horst, M., Kirby, D. A., & Lewenstein, B. (2019). Science stories as culture: experience, identity, narrative and emotion in public communication of science. *Journal of Science Communication, 18*(5).

Dickinson, P., Gilbert, J., Higgins, A., St, Matthew., Pierre, P., Solomon, D., Zwagerman, S., Barreca, R., Bratton, J., Bush-Bailey, G., & Colletta, L.

(2014). *Women and comedy: History, theory, practice.* Fairleigh Dickinson University Press.

Flicker, E. (2008). Women scientists in mainstream film: social role models—Contribution to the public understanding of science from the perspective of film sociology. In P. Weingart & B. Hüppauf (Eds.), *Science Images and Popular Images of the Sciences,* (pp. 241–256). Routledge.

Fogg-Rogers, L., & Hobbs. L. (2019). Catch 22—Improving visibility of women in science and engineering for both recruitment and retention. *Journal of Science Communication, 18*(4), C05. https://doi.org/10.22323/2.180 40305

Geena Davis Institute on Gender in Media. (2018). The "Scully effect": I want to believe ... in STEM. Geena Davis Institute on Gender in Media https://seejane.org/wp-content/uploads/x-files-scully-effect-rep ort-geena-davis-institute.pdf

Gorp, B. V., Rommes, E. W. M., & Emons, P. A. A. (2014). From the wizard to the doubter. Prototypes of scientists and engineers in fiction and non-fiction media aimed at dutch children and teenagers. *Public Understanding of Science, 23*(6), 646–659. https://doi.org/10.1177/0963662512468566

Haynes, R. (2003). From alchemy to artificial intelligence: Stereotypes of the scientist in Western literature. *Public Understanding of Science, 12*(3), 243–253. https://doi.org/10.1177/0963662503123003

Haynes, R. D. (2016). Whatever happened to the 'mad, bad' scientist? Overturning the stereotype. *Public Understanding of Science, 25*(1), 31–44. https://doi.org/10.1177/0963662514535689

Helmer, M., Schottdorf, M., Neef, A., & Battaglia, D. (2017). Gender bias in scholarly peer review. *eLife, 6,* 1–18. https://doi.org/10.7554/eLife.21718

Hüppauf, B., & Weingart, P. (2007). Images in and of science. In B. Hüppauf & P. Weingart (Eds.), *Science Images and Popular Images of the Sciences,* (pp. 3–31). Taylor & Francis Group.

Hyde, J. S., Bigler, R. S., Joel, D., Tate, C. C., & van Anders, S. M. (2019). The future of sex and gender in psychology: Five challenges to the gender binary. *American Psychologist, 74*(2), 171–193. https://doi.org/10.1037/amp0000307

Johnson, A. M. (1992). Language ability and sex affect humor appreciation. *Perceptual and Motor Skills, 75*(2), 571–581. https://doi.org/10.2466/pms.1992.75.2.571

Johnston, J. C. (2014). Taking humour seriously: women and the theatre of virginie ancelot. *Nottingham French Studies, 53*(3), 267–284. https://doi.org/10.3366/nfs.2014.0092

Jones, R. A. (1997). The boffin. A stereotype of scientists in post-war british films (1945–1970). *Public Understanding of Science, 6*(1), 31–48. https://doi.org/10.1088/0963-6625/6/1/003

Jones, T. M., Fanson, K. V., Lanfear, R., Symonds, M. R. E., & Megan Higgie, M. (2014). Gender differences in conference presentations: a consequence of self-selection? *PeerJ*, *1*, 1–16. https://doi.org/10.7717/peerj.627

Jontes, D., & Trdina, A. (2018). Ridiculing the working-class body in post-socialist sitcom. *Comedy Studies*, *9*(1), 50–62. https://doi.org/10.1080/204 0610X.2018.1437165

Jürgens, A.-S. (2021). Lady clowns: Clown-Ballerinas, dancing 'Clownesses' and female clowns on the popular stage around 1900. In G. Bush-Bailey, & K. Flaherty (Eds.), *Touring Performance and Global Exchange 1850–1960: Making Tracks*. Routledge.

Kaltenbacher, M., & Drews, S. (2020). An inconvenient joke? A review of humor in climate change communication. *Environmental Communication*, *14*(6), 717–729. https://doi.org/10.1080/17524032.2020.1756888

Kellner, D. (2020). *Media culture: Cultural studies, identity, and politics in the contemporary moment*. Taylor & Francis.

Kirby, D. A. (2008). Cinematic Science. In M. Bucchi & B. Trench (Eds.), *Handbook of Public Communication of Science and Technology*, (pp. 41–57). Routledge.

Kirby, D. A. (2017). The changing popular images of science. In K. H. Jamieson, D. M. Kahan, D. A. Scheufele (Eds.), *The Oxford Handbook of the Science of Science Communication*, (pp. 291–298). Oxford Handbooks Online. https://doi.org/10.1093/oxfordhb/9780190497620.013.32

Knobloch-Westerwick, S., Glynn, C. J., & Huge, M. (2013). The matilda effect in science communication: An experiment on gender bias in publication quality perceptions and collaboration interest. *Science Communication*, *35*(5), 603–625. https://doi.org/10.1177/1075547012472684

Kuipers, G. (2006). *Good humor, bad taste: A sociology of the joke* (Vol. 7). De Gruyter Mouton. https://doi.org/10.1515/9783110898996

Lawler, A. (1996). Goldin puts NASA on new trajectory. *Science*, *272*(5263), 800. https://doi.org/10.1126/science.272.5263.800

Lincoln, A. E., Pincus, S., Bandows Koster, J., & Leboy, P. S. (2012). The Matilda effect in science: Awards and prizes in the US, 1990s and 2000s. *Social Studies of Science*, *42*(2), 307–320. https://doi.org/10.1177/030631 2711435830

Locke, S. (2005). Fantastically reasonable: Ambivalence in the representation of science and technology in super-hero comics. *Public Understanding of Science*, *14*(1), 25–46. https://doi.org/10.1177/0963662505048197

Lockyer, S. (2011). From toothpick legs to dropping vaginas: Gender and sexuality in Joan Rivers' stand-up comedy performance. *Comedy Studies*, *2*(2), 113–123. https://doi.org/10.1386/cost.2.2.113_1

Lockyer, S. (2020). Women and comedy. In K. Ross, I. Bachmann, V. Cardo, S. Moorti & M. Scarcelli (Eds.) *The International Encyclopedia of Gender,*

Media, and Communication, (pp. 1–7). Wiley. https://doi.org/10.1002/978 1119429128.iegmc237

Longo, M. (2010). Humour use and knowledge-making at the margins. *Canadian Social Work Review*, *27*(1), 113–126.

McIntosh, H. (2014). Representations of female scientists in the big bang theory. *Journal of Popular Film and Television*, *42*(4), 195–204. https://doi.org/10. 1080/01956051.2014.896779

O'Meara, D. J., & Monaghan, W. (2024). Lesbian, gay, bisexual, transgender, and nonbinary representation on Australian scripted television in the 2000s and 2010s. *Media International Australia*, 1329878X241236990. https://doi.org/10.1177/1329878X241236990

Pansegrau, P. (2008). Stereotypes and images of scientists in fiction films. In P. Weingart & B. Hüppauf (Eds.), *Science Images and Popular Images of Science*, (pp. 33–51). Routledge. https://doi.org/10.4324/9780203939154-17

Pinto, B., Marçal, D., & Vaz, S. G. (2015). Communicating through humour. A project of stand-up comedy about science. *Public Understanding of Science*, *24*(7), 776–793. https://doi.org/10.1177/0963662513511175

Rhodes, N. & Ellithorpe, M. E. (2016). Laughing at risk: Sitcom laugh tracks communicate norms for behavior. *Media Psychology*, *19*(3), 359–380.

Riesch, H. (2015). Why did the proton cross the road? Humour and science communication. *Public Understanding of Science*, *24*(7), 768–775. https://doi.org/10.1177/0963662514546299

Rioux, C., Paré, A., London-Nadeau, K., Juster, R.-P., Weedon, S., Levasseur-Puhach, S., Freeman, M., Roos, L. E., & Tomfohr-Madsen, L. M. (2022). Sex and gender terminology: A glossary for gender-inclusive epidemiology. *Journal of Epidemiology and Community Health*, *76*(8), 764–768. https://doi.org/10.1136/jech-2022-219171

Riquelme, A. R., Carretero-Dios, H., Megías, J. L., & Romero-Sánchez, M. (2023). Subversive humor against sexism: Conceptualization and first evidence on its empirical nature. *Current Psychology*, *42*(19), 16208–16221. https://doi.org/10.1007/s12144-019-00331-9

Rossiter, M. W. (1993). The Matilda effect in science. *Social Studies of Science*, *23*(2), 325–341. https://doi.org/10.1177/030631293023002004

Simis-Wilkinson, M., Madden, H., Lassen, D., Su., Yi-Fan, & L., Brossard, D., Scheufele, D. A., & Xenos, M. A. (2018). Scientists joking on social media: An empirical analysis of #overlyhonestmethods. *Science Communication*, *40*(3), 314–339. https://doi.org/10.1177/1075547018766557

Soucy-Humphreys, J., Judd, K., & Jürgens, A.-S. (2023). Challenging the stereotype through humor? Comic female scientists in animated TV series for young audiences. *Frontiers in Communication*, *7*, 1024602. https://doi.org/10.3389/fcomm.2022.1024602

Steinke, J. (1999). Women scientist role models on screen: A case study of Contact. *Science Communication, 21*(2), 111–136. https://doi.org/10. 1177/1075547099021002002

Steinke, J. (2005). Cultural representations of gender and science: Portrayals of female scientists and engineers in popular films. *Science Communication, 27*(1), 27–63. https://doi.org/10.1177/1075547005278610

Steinke, J. (2012). Portrayals of female scientists in the mass media. In A.N. Valdivia (Ed.), *The International Encyclopedia of Media Studies*. Wiley. https://doi.org/10.1002/9781444361506.wbiems070

Subramaniapillai, S., Galea, L. A. M., Einstein, G., & de Lange, A.-M. G. (2024). Sex and gender in health research: Intersectionality matters. *Frontiers in Neuroendocrinology, 72*, 101104. https://doi.org/10.1016/j.yfrne.2023. 101104

Terzian, S. G., & Grunzke, A. L. (2007). Scrambled eggheads: Ambivalent representations of scientists in six Hollywood film comedies from 1961 to 1965. *Public Understanding of Science, 16*(4), 407–419. https://doi.org/10.1177/ 0963662506067908

Villegas Simón, I., Sánchez Soriano, J. J., & Ventura, R. (2024). 'If you don't "pass" as cis, you don't exist'. The trans audience's reproofs of 'Cis Gaze' and transnormativity in TV series. *European Journal of Communication, 39*(1), 22–36. https://doi.org/10.1177/02673231231163704

Willey, A., & Subramaniam, B. (2017). Inside the social world of asocials: White nerd masculinity, science, and the politics of reverent disdain. *Feminist Studies, 43*(1), 13–41. https://doi.org/10.1353/fem.2017.0010

"Oh the Team Had Thoughts, but You Know, 'Misogyny, Misogyny'": Research Context

Abstract This chapter of *Women Scientists in American Television Comedy: Beakers, Big Bangs and Broken Hearts* reviews existing literature examining the persistent underrepresentation of women in STEM fields and how television portrayals contribute to this disparity. We highlight how cultural stereotypes present science as a masculine pursuit, where women scientists are frequently depicted through limiting narratives that prioritize traditional gender roles, personal conflicts and diminished competence. Such portrayals can influence public perceptions and discourage young women from pursuing STEM careers. The chapter delves into the impact of humor as both a reinforcing and challenging force in these portrayals. By framing women scientists as sources of comic relief, TV shows risk trivializing their professional identities, which can perpetuate stereotypes. However, the chapter also explores how comedy has the potential to disrupt these norms, offering viewers alternative, empowering representations of women in STEM. An intersectional perspective is considered in how media portrayals affect not only women but also marginalized groups in STEM. We address how the use of ironic and feminist humor in popular media can activate audience reflection on gender norms, supporting broader engagement and cultural change. Through an examination of humor's role in representation, this chapter sheds light on the complexities of gender, STEM and media influence,

K. Judd et al., *Women Scientists in American Television Comedy*, Palgrave Studies in Science and Popular Culture, https://doi.org/10.1007/978-3-031-81525-6_2

underscoring humor's power to challenge stereotypes and foster positive shifts in how women scientists are perceived in American television.

Keywords Gender stereotypes · Cultural perception of science · Media representation of women scientists · TV comedy and science

Why is it that women are still so underrepresented in STEM? We explore what portrayals of women scientist stereotypes in the media might have something to do with this and how humor holds great power to promote positive engagement and change within STEM spaces; so in the real workplace there might be less of "oh the team had thoughts, but you know, 'misogyny, misogyny'" (*Zoey's Extraordinary Failure*, S01E5).

Underrepresentation of Women in STEM

Despite global trends of girls outperforming boys in most school contexts, boys have been found to be more confident in their science skills compared to other areas such as reading and literacy (Mostafa, 2019; Parker et al., 2018). While women made up 47% of the total US workforce in 2021, a significant gender gap exists in STEM disciplines, where women only comprised 35% of the science and engineering workforce (National Science Board, 2024). Although the underrepresentation of women in STEM is persistent globally (Bello et al., 2021), it is not equal in all areas of science. Young women in many countries around the world do tend to study for and aspire to careers in fields such as biology, environmental science and health in greater proportions than other areas of STEM such as computer sciences, physics, mathematics and engineering (Sikora, 2019). In the United States, there are relatively high proportions of women with a bachelor's degree in social sciences (65%) and life sciences (48%), and fewer women in physical sciences (35%), computer and mathematical sciences (26%) and engineering (16%) (National Science Board, 2022).

The reasons for women's historical and continued exclusion from science are multifaceted, intersecting and pervasive from a young age (Bian et al., 2017; Dehdarirad et al., 2015; Halpern et al., 2007; Rosser, 2018), with much literature on the topic showing complexity and nuance through contradiction (Ceci & Williams, 2011; Ceci et al.,

2014; Dehdarirad et al., 2015). Some of these reasons include but are not limited to: stereotypes of science (discussed in more detail below) as a masculine pursuit (e.g. Carli et al., 2016; Institute of Medicine, 2007), expectations on women to perform traditional gender roles both inside and outside the workplace (Sassler et al., 2017), structural barriers to women's retention and progression (e.g. Miner et al., 2018), women's lower familiarity with and self-efficacy in STEM (Cheryan et al., 2017) and perceptions of science as incompatible with femininity and feminine identities (Archer et al., 2012; Dawson et al., 2020; Francis et al., 2017; Starr, 2018). Research regarding the experiences of other groups traditionally minoritized in STEM (including people of color and people from non-English speaking backgrounds or low socio-economic status) is a growing area of research in sciences and Science Communication in recent years, especially in the US and UK (see e.g. Judd & McKinnon, 2021; Nelson & Cheng, 2018). Studies using an intersectional framework to examine how minoritized people navigate the interface and, often, conflicts, between their identities and science culture (see Medin & Bang, 2014 on science culture) is similarly a growing area of interest (Judd & McKinnon, 2021; Rodrigues et al., 2023). Empowering stories from African women in STEM illustrate this uphill battle of pursuing STEM in low resource settings as a woman, where the cultural belief is that "your first responsibility is to be a mother. Anything else beyond that? Well, good luck to you, even if you have an understanding partner" (Powell, 2022, p. 710). Against this background, stereotypical representations of women scientists play an important role in reflecting, if not fostering, the underrepresentation of women in STEM and in promoting ideologies of gender and gender roles—and this also applies to such depictions in the media.

STEREOTYPING OF WOMEN IN STEM

Stereotypes regarding the suitability of women in scientific careers arise from cultural understandings of what it means to be feminine and what it means to be a scientist (Francis et al., 2017), especially in a Western cultural context (Thébaud & Charles, 2018). Conversely, stereotypes around science center on natural genius, singular focus and mechanical aptitude—qualities prized in Western masculinity (Cheryan et al., 2015). The perception of science as masculine, and its subsequent marginalization of women, has been the interest of academics for decades, with Kelly (1985) identifying four distinct senses in which science is masculine, including the greater proportions of men in science, packaging of science in a way that connects with the interests and motivations of men, gender differences in science education that restrict learning for girls, and the sense that science is inherently masculine given its social construction in a patriarchal society. Rasekoala (2019, p. 2) identified science communication as a "ghetto" of women, a space that is "lower paid, less status, [with] less stability" (Lewenstein, 2019, p. 2) compared to science, perceived as the more 'masculine' pursuit—a binary largely based in these gendered stereotypes.

Research has shown that children form gender stereotypes around intellectual ability early, having impacts that continue later in life (Bian et al., 2017). Miller et al. (2015) correlated women's participation in science with the prevalence of gender-science stereotypes in 66 nations. Women themselves are not immune to believing and perpetuating negative stereotypes about women in science, calling their peers "bitchy", "bossy", "too pretty" or even "bad at science", among other phrases (McKinnon & O'Connell, 2020, p. 5). However, even positive-sounding stereotypes of women in science can belie more negative assumptions. Stereotypes of women in STEM as more "maternal" (e.g. McKinnon & O'Connell, 2020, p. 5) or as being "sweet", "nice" or "morally purer than men" can still have undesirable impacts (Kuchynka et al., 2018, p. 77). Stereotypes, in addition to the (numerical) underrepresentation of women in STEM careers, can affect women's confidence and engagement in the STEM workplace (van Veelen et al., 2019). However, acting "more masculine" is not necessarily the answer, with further hurdles potentially arising from non-gender-conforming behavior (O'Connell & McKinnon, 2021). Additionally, research—especially from the United States—indicates that this is an intersectional issue with Indigenous People and People of Color also suffering from unsupportive stereotypes regarding their participation in STEM (e.g. Eaton et al., 2020; O'Brien et al., 2015). It is important to note that even though stereotypes portray science as a masculinized pursuit, there is no consistent evidence that men are inherently better at science (Charles, 2011). Despite this, engaging with negative stereotypes can produce measurable underperformance—an effect known as "stereotype threat" (Steele, 1997). For young women, this stereotype threat can lead to poorer academic performance due to de-identification with the domain from which the negative stereotype is derived (Steele, 1997). Such negative stereotypes that pose a threat for

women in STEM have historically pervaded mass media when women
have been represented in such domains.

Underrepresentation
of Women Scientists in Media

The representation of women in media mirrors what society deems as
culturally acceptable positions for women to assume and how women
scientist stereotypes are perceived in cultural contexts (Flicker, 2008,
p. 243; Steinke 2005, p. 28 on the definition of the cinematic mode
of "representation"; Fogg-Rogers, 2017). Scholarly research concerning
the portrayal of women scientists in the media has identified that, until
recently, they have been largely underrepresented in comparison to their
male counterparts. This finding is consistent across newspapers, magazines, film and television (Clark & Illman, 2006; LaFollette, 1988; Long
et al., 2010; Steinke 2005). Non-fictional women scientists in the media
are less frequently represented than their male counterparts (Price &
Payne, 2019), with this underrepresentation often going unquestioned
(e.g. Yong, 2018). Although this underrepresentation reflects the statis-
tical gender disparity in STEM professions, it is also indicative of the
cultural bias of STEM as a masculine domain (Banchefsky et al., 2016;
LaFollette, 1988). A study exploring coverage from 2011 to 2018 of the
"Profiles in Science" column of "The Science Times" showed progress,
with 12 profiles of women scientists compared to 18 male scientists
(Mitchell & McKinnon, 2019, p. 181)—this is in comparison to a study
of coverage from 1980 to 2000 which only identified 16 women scientists out of the 203 scientists featured (Clark & Illman, 2006), indicating
that while there is progress in women's representation, it is both small
and slow. In fictional contexts, earlier studies of popular films from 1991
to 2001 also identified an underrepresentation of women scientists with
only 25 out of 75 films having a woman, rather than a man, scientist
or engineer as the lead character (Steinke, 2005). Further analysis of
popular films between 2002 and 2014 reported this "symbolic annihilation" (Tuchman, 2000, p. 150) of women scientists in film with a ratio
of 2 to 1 men to women scientists (Steinke, 2017). Soucy-Humphreys
et al. (2023) found instances of this symbolic annihilation in the portrayal
of women scientists in animated children's television, relying heavily on
archaic stereotypes about gender performance and presentation. In the
medium of mainstream comics, comic women scientists have only recently

been explored through the prism of symmetry, a concept allowing for a better understanding of how scientific logics and practices influence and enable the transformation of a woman scientist into a clown, in this case Dr Harleen Quinzel (aka Harley Quinn), thus challenging women scientist identities (Santos & Jürgens, 2023).

Ideologies of Gender and STEM in Media

Where women scientists have been represented in mass media, their portrayal has been reported as problematic and consistent with depictions of women working in other professions, involving traditional gender stereotypes that place a heavy emphasis on femininity and beauty, romantic or interpersonal relations, dependency on men and family life (Steinke, 2012). Negative women scientist stereotypes were typically reinforced in the media by downplaying expertise of women scientists, emphasizing conflicts between personal and professional lives and suggesting that masculine skills and traits are necessary to engage in scientific research (Steinke, 1997; the implications of the cultural construction of science through media in relation to gender are discussed in more detail in Brewer & Ley, 2022, pp. 11–20). Earlier portrayals of women scientists in magazines and newspapers portray a dichotomous narrative, where they are perceived as either extraordinary and unusual "superscientists", or a subordinate assistant (LaFollette, 1988, p. 270). Unlike those of male scientists, representations in media also place a heavy emphasis on the domestic duties of women scientists and their challenges in pursuing a career and maintaining traditional maternal roles (LaFollette, 1988; Mitchell & McKinnon, 2019). Studies of the articles of scientists in the "Science Times" from 1996 to 1997, identified that those of women scientists had a gender-based narrative rather than the scientific-narrative of articles on male scientists (Shachar, 2000). Articles on women scientists also had a dominant focus placed on the apparent "dilemma of being a woman in science" and suggest that the scientist's main source of empowerment is derived from her status as a mother (Shachar, 2000, p. 352). While a recent study of two American media outlets found that some gender and broader stereotypes about scientists were beginning to be challenged in non-fiction media profiles of scientists, many continue to be reinforced (Benson-Greenwald et al., 2022). Yet public sentiment about the portrayal of women as scientists in fiction media is still mixed. For example, while Twitter conversations about female Marvel superheroes showed gendered criticism (Griffin, 2022), Twitter discourse about women scientist characters in science fiction blockbuster movies was previously found to be relatively neutral (Simis et al., 2015). A content analysis of 14 television programs popular among school-aged children also commented on the disproportionate representation of women scientists but found that the depictions across the genders concerning professional position, marital status and parental status were generally consistent (Long et al., 2010). Looking more broadly at women characters in different occupations across a variety of television genres, Hohestein and Thalman (2019) discovered that the way that women in American television were represented changed throughout the 2010s. They found that women characters gained more depth and complexity, with more recent productions more likely to challenge sexist stereotypes and engage in feminist discourse—a change they attributed to broader cultural change, as well as more diversity in television production personnel. However, a study of women scientist characters in the animated children's shows *Adventure Time* and *Spongebob Squarepants* found that while they were presented as complex and multidimensional characters, they still fell into classic archetypes (cf. Flicker, 2008) where they needed to be supported and even rescued by the men around them (Soucy-Humphreys et al., 2023). Moreover, their scientific prowess was diminished through illustrations of their achievements being more akin to magic, and the source of humor related to the female characters, as opposed to their less competent male acquaintances who achieved their success through luck and hard work, and could be inherently humorous (Soucy-Humpreys et al., 2023). Soucy-Humphreys et al. (2023) concluded that while great strides have been made in the representation of fictional women scientists, the ways that hegemonic binary gender norms are used in fictional media have considerable room for improvement.

The recurring portrayal of stereotypes across multiple media platforms contributes to the credibility and normalization of hegemonic gender roles (Lauzen et al., 2008, p. 201). With the public normally having little to no personal interaction with working scientists in day-to-day contexts beyond popular science or other science communication types (Scheufele, 2013), normalizing negative stereotypical perceptions in media can not only be damaging to public trust in science but also influence women and young girls perception and consideration of a career in STEM (Mitchell & McKinnon, 2019, pp. 177–178). For example, a study around the film *Hidden Figures*, released in 2016 but portraying a US scientific and cultural environment in the 1960s, found that after viewing the film, female preservice teachers believed that while women could become scientists, mathematicians and engineers and contribute to societal progress, women would not be welcomed into the STEM workplace (Yıldırım et al., 2021). Another study identified that many women currently working in STEM identified the female protagonist of *The X-Files*, Dana Scully, as a personal role model and influential figure to pursue STEM (Geena Davis Institute on Gender in Media, 2018). This has been termed "The Scully Effect" and emphasizes the importance of positive fictional STEM role models. Further, Pietri et al. (2021) spotlighted the importance of positive visual portrayals of women scientists to promote uptake of STEM careers by Black women. The study reported that Black female students had a stronger connection and greater interest in computer science after viewing a video presentation of a Black female computer scientist in comparison to reading an identical written transcript, thus highlighting the importance of rich audiovisual representation and diversity in popular films and TV shows (Pietri et al., 2021). Within this context, it is interesting to note that scholars in the field of Media Psychology have studied the way humor and identification with characters may influence audience behavior, including the activation of communicated norms (focusing on sitcoms, Rhodes & Ellithorpe, 2016; see Kalviknes, 2010 on audience assumptions about femininity and comedic performance). Indeed, humor in the form of comedy is an effective tool to transmit not only the content of a message but also the values and social identities embedded in it (Lockyer & Pickering, 2008), with research showing that the rebellious nature of humor can enable TV comedies to shape, if not challenge, social and cultural norms (Mackie, 1990).

WOMEN AND HUMOR

Like science, comic performance has long been considered a masculine pursuit (Dickinson et al., 2014; Johnston, 2014; Lockyer, 2020), with the participation of women marginalized in the production and consumption of comedy (Johnston, 2014). Rather than having an active role, women were more often the target (Dickinson et al., 2014), with ideas of women's 'hysteria' often close by (Mizejewski & Sturtevant, 2017). Women have tended to be the objects of desire, disdain or derision in jokes, with their image and relationship to men, rather than their inner perspective, their service to comedy—think of 'dumb blonde' or 'mean mother-in-law' jokes (Kuipers, 2006). Indeed much comedy about gender, especially in recent decades, has relied on tropes of the 'natural differences' between men and women (Bemiller & Schneider, 2010)—the "Mars and Venus" dichotomy described by Shifman and Lemish (2011, p. 253) in their analysis of online jokes. Men in the gender-based jokes they studied were often immature buffoons, while "complicated and smart" 'modern women' made their lives unbearable (Shifman & Lemish, 2011). While men and women can both be the butt of gender-based jokes, the way that they are characterized in humor is often different, reinforcing traditional, sexist and binary stereotypes (Shifman & Lemish, 2010). However, humor is both complex and subjective, and feminist readings—and amusement—can be found in even sexist comedy (Sunderland, 2007).

Women who dare to be funny have often been dismissed as unruly or otherwise problematic (Rowe, 1995). Frances Gray (1994) illustrates that dismissing women as 'not funny' was an intentional act of silencing women's voices, and a myth that reaches back at least as far as the seventeenth century. Dismissing women as 'not being able to take a joke' has similarly been deployed to shut down feminist criticism of sexist humor (Gill, 2011), even making feminists the butt the joke themselves by portraying them as humorless, unfeminine, 'feminazis' (Bergman, 1986; Gill, 2007). These jokes continue today in new mediums such as memes online, where the 'humorous' format is an attempt to shield the underlying misogyny (Drakett et al., 2018; Worth et al., 2016), especially through ironic sexism (Drakett et al., 2018; Quart, 2012). Quart (2012) contends that ironic sexism objectifies through mockery of women's bodies and sexuality. The irony arises from how 'edgy' it is that such egregious sexism is casually being said aloud—but of course, the manipulation is that 'we're all in on the joke' (Gill, 2007). Ironic sexist humor at once takes feminism for granted and tears it down from behind (Benwell, 2007; Gill, 2007), relying on an assumption that feminism has resulted in gender equity in society (Bemiller & Schneider, 2010; Quart, 2012; Sunderland, 2007)—which is provably false (e.g. United Nations Department of Economic & Social Affairs, 2023). As Greenwood and Isbell (2002, p. 348) remark, "sexist humor behaves like any other form of discrimination. It may be even more dangerous, in fact, for its deceptively light, good-natured packaging". Benwell (2007) describes ironic sexism as slippery *because* it can be interpreted in different ways by different audiences. In this way, ironic sexism is a case of "having it both ways"—being grossly sexist while claiming one doesn't actually 'mean it' (Gill, 2007, p. 159). Experimental evidence has shown that people exposed to sexist jokes are more likely to accept sexist beliefs (Ford et al., 2013), feel more justified in their own sexist beliefs (Ford et al., 2001), and more likely to withhold support for feminist causes (Ford et al., 2008). While women also have been observed using humor to perpetuate sexist humor online (Bartlett et al., 2014), women continue to be silenced and diminished through threats and misogyny delivered as 'just a joke' (Cole, 2015) in an attempt—conscious or not—to appear less confrontational and violent (Mallett et al., 2016). However, Bergman (1986) argues that the intention of a sexist joke doesn't matter, because it is still likely to cause harm to those already impacted by sexism. Importantly, those impacts can occur not just to the individual, but societally (Woodzicka & Ford, 2010).

Feminists aren't just the target of jokes, though. Riquelme et al. (2023) define 'feminist humor' as a subversive style that critiques society—as opposed to simply ridiculing men. Bing (2004) argues that feminist humor is by, for and about women's shared experiences, power and perspective. And while aforementioned experiments with sexist humor show increased sexism, exposure to subversive, feminist humor was more likely to lead to participating in collective action supporting feminist ideals (Riquelme et al., 2021).

The stereotype of women's place as protagonists in comedy is changing. Women's historical and contemporary role in comedy—and indeed comedy's role in the advancement of feminism—are beginning to be uncovered and acknowledged (Hennefeld, 2017; Mizejewski & Sturtevant, 2017). While many of today's 'big names' of women in comedy are still white, and their brand of feminism similarly white (cf. Christensen, 1997; see also Colpean and Tully (2019) for discussion of 'feminist comedy' being used, for example, to distract from racism), many other *comediennes* use their work to subvert and explore the taboo (Holmes, 2017). Likewise, feminist scholar bell hooks[1] called for comedy to be used as a tool of intersectional political activism (hooks, 2014), a call which has been heeded by many women of color who push the boundaries of performance to embody their whole identities (Blackburn, 2018). Feminist humor is important because, as Mizejewski and Sturtevant (2017,

---

[1] The styling of bell hooks' name in lower case is deliberate, following the precedent of hooks herself, who argued that her name was less important than her words. See Smith (2022) for further discussion of hooks' life and work.

p. 4) point out, it can "help reverse social myths that a woman's proper or natural role is to appreciate male humor rather than speak her own truth through comedy". The same is true of other marginalized voices, in that comedy can be a vehicle to speak truth to power through subversive comedy (Saucier et al., 2018), to express identity and lived experience both within and beyond community, and, importantly, to find and convey joy (Osbourne, 2023). Mizejewski and Sturtevant (2017) also make a case for more spaces where women's voices in comedy are intentionally emphasized. Intentional and holistic inclusion, rather than an 'add women and stir' approach is critical, as Weber (2017) demonstrated that quotas for women comedians on British panel shows did nothing to address the underlying factors for their earlier exclusion.

HUMOR, THE COMMUNICATION OF SCIENCE AND COMEDIC PORTRAYALS OF WOMEN STEM PROFESSIONALS IN TV

Over the past centuries, numerous theories have been proposed to explain what humor is and how it can be defined, without a clear consensus among humor theorists as to which of these three theories is most viable. The major humor theories are Relief Theory (which argues that humor is a means of relieving tension by expressing ideas that are inappropriate in serious discourse), Superiority Theory (which interprets humor as an expression of the superiority of the one doing the humor over their target) and Incongruity Theory (which encompasses a variety of theories that link the humorous effect to the unexpected ending of a humorous text that is nevertheless consistent with its structure; Meyer, 2000; Morreall, 2016). Many other humor forms have been developed and discussed such as sexist humor or feminist humor (Shifman & Lemish, 2010).

One of the main features that make contemporary humor so attractive is its transmedial visuality and entertainment value (Jürgens et al., 2021). However, humor is not just an attractive representation strategy, it is also an effective rhetorical device. Meyer (2000), for example, looks at how humor demarcates group identity and negotiates social norms by outlining four communicative functions of humor: identification, clarification, enforcement and differentiation. The role of humor and comedy, particularly in communicating scientific information to different publics, has been studied in various realms of science, science education and science communication by Hee et al. (2022), Yeo et al. (2020), Skurka et al. (2019), among many others. Humor, as shown in research on classroom settings, can positively impact student learning and classroom experience (e.g. Cooper et al., 2018; Kobayashi & Berge, 2022), but it is also a double-edged sword. Important publications by Kaltenbacher and Drews (2020), Bangsund (2018) and O'Neill and Nicholson-Cole (2009), for example, highlight the ambivalence of humor in the context of climate change understanding and action. In climate messaging, humor has been shown to deepen audience perception of messages and motivate environmental activism (Skurka et al., 2018). Osnes et al. (2019 p. 224) investigate how "good-natured comedy" helps people "positively process negative emotions" regarding global threats, sustain hope and grow as communicators themselves. Humor can generate positive emotions such as joy (in the producer and receiver), which is not to be underestimated, because joy feeds hope—and hope is essential for sustained action (Osnes et al., 2019). However, while exploring the role of humor in engaging audiences around scientific information and science-based issues, these and many other studies (e.g. Yeo et al., 2020) do not consider the relevance of broader cultural narratives of science.

What most of these studies do highlight, though, is the genuine ambivalence—the pitfalls and promises—of humor more generally. Humor can draw attention to scientific topics and increase interest and engagement with them (Anderson & Becker, 2018; Eisend, 2009), but it can also distract people's attention from the main message and negatively affect the credibility of serious issues (Pinto et al., 2015; Pinto & Riesch, 2015; Riesch, 2015). Maybe not surprisingly, humor is dismissed as trivial (Lockyer & Pickering, 2008), which is why humorously framed messages might not be perceived as equally important as the ones expressed seriously (Grugulis, 2002, p. 388). It may also risk trivializing serious issues and impede behavioral action (Kaltenbacher & Drews, 2020). Among the complex intricacies of humor (see, e.g., Bore & Reid, 2014), humorous statements often allow for multiple and even conflicting interpretations due to its subjective nature. Humor can promote positive engagement with serious and laughing matters, but only if it is actually perceived as funny. The choice of a particular interpretation over others also depends on the general cultural context and the particular circumstances of a communicative event (Pickering & Lockyer, 2005, p. 9). Within this context, Science Communication scholars have explored the influence of sitcoms on audience perceptions and attitudes toward science and scientists, including the role of women scientists (Li, 2016, pp. 123–135)—with a focus on *The Big Bang Theory*.

Given its success across over 30 countries, there has been substantial research into the production and content of the humor used in *The Big Bang Theory* in particular. Previous studies have explored the production and interpretation of verbal humor in *The Big Bang Theory* in terms of cognition and communication through various pragmatic theories, including Ran Yongping's (2004) adaptation-relevance model (Ma & Jiang, 2013) and Sperber and Wilson's (1995) relevance theory (Sartika & Pranoto, 2021). Rosie White investigates the queer potential of eccentric masculinities in *The Big Bang Theory* (2018, Chapter 3); Dave Zobel (2015) and Mark Brake (2019) explain the science of the series. Under the adaptation-relevance model, *The Big Bang Theory* creates humor when the audiences seek optimal relevance from the character's utterances, interpreting linguistic and contextual cues to achieve successful communication culminating in amusement and humorous effects (Ma & Jiang, 2013, p. 2226). Using relevance theory, Sartika and Pranoto (2021) identified that the mechanism of humor in the sitcom is through a moment of optimal relevance of cognitive principle, whereby the audience's presumption of the context of the conversation is contradicted by something unexpected, producing humorous effects (Sartika & Pranoto, 2021). A previous textual analysis of *The Big Bang Theory* identified two dominant language styles used to elicit a humor response: hyperbole and sarcasm (Pramita, 2021, p. 73). Conversations featuring these humor styles, most commonly including the male scientists, were packaged in scientific terms (Pramita, 2021, p. 73). Instances of sarcasm often involve one of the main male scientists' (Sheldon) inability to read sarcasm due to his need to rationalize all things, thereby inviting laughter from the audience who easily read the sarcastic tones presented (Pramita, 2021, p. 73). Nuances of humor are triggered as the scientists are "considered inferior, different from usual and strange at the same time" (Pramita, 2021, p. 73). Less of the humor analysis is focused on that of the series' two women scientists, Amy and Bernadette (cf. McIntosh, 2014, p. 196; the lack of discussion also applies to the women protagonists of other contemporary comedy series such as *Never Have I Ever* and *Zoey's Extraordinary Playlist*). The present study is the first investigation into the gender-based portrayals of science characters in *Never Have I Ever* and *Zoey's Extraordinary Playlist* in the context of humor. Overall, our approach to these TV shows follows Eva Flicker's (2008, p. 241) understanding of stereotypes, media and their representational function: "media take more liberties in the construction of pictures of reality, yet their reference system nonetheless remains, more or less, social reality". For our investigation of the specific humor in the 'construction of pictures of reality' and comedic portrayals of women scientists in television shows we draw from and expand on a humor typology published in 2004 by Moniek Buijzen and Patti M. Valkenburg.

REFERENCES

Anderson, A. A., & Becker, A. B. (2018). Not just funny after all: Sarcasm as a catalyst for public engagement with climate change. *Science Communication, 40*(4), 524–540. https://doi.org/10.1177/1075547018786560

Archer, L., Dewitt, J., Osborne, J., Dillon, J., Willis, B., & Wong, B. (2012). 'Balancing acts': Elementary school girls' negotiations of femininity, achievement, and science. *Science Education, 96*(6), 967–989. https://doi.org/10.1002/sce.21031

Banchefsky, S., Westfall, J., Park, B., & Judd, C. (2016). But you don't look like a scientist!: Women scientists with feminine appearance are deemed less likely to be scientists. *Sex Roles, 75*(3–4), 95–109. https://doi.org/10.1007/s11199-016-0586-1

Bangsund, A. D. (2018). *Having a laugh? The role of humour in adolescents' climate change communication* (Doctoral dissertation, Royal Roads University (Canada)). https://viurrspace.ca/bitstream/handle/10613/5664/Bangsund_royalroads_1313O_10520.pdf

Bartlett, J., Norrie, R., Patel, S., Rumpel, R., & Wibberley, S. (2014). *Misogyny on Twitter*. Demos. https://demos.co.uk/wp-content/uploads/2014/05/MISOGYNY_ON_TWITTER.pdf

Bello, A., Blowers, T., Schneegans, S., & Straza, T. (2021). To be smart, the digital revolution will need to be inclusive. *UNESCO Science Report: The race against time for smarter development*. https://unesdoc.unesco.org/ark:/48223/pf0000375429

Bemiller, M. L., & Schneider, R. Z. (2010). It's not just a joke. *Sociological Spectrum, 30*(4), 459–479. https://doi.org/10.1080/02732171003641040

Benson-Greenwald, T. M., Joshi, M. P., & Diekman, A. B. (2022). Out of the lab and into the world: analyses of social roles and gender in profiles of scientists in the New York times and the scientist. *Frontiers in Psychology, 12*. https://doi.org/10.3389/fpsyg.2021.684777

Benwell, B. (2007). New sexism? *Journalism Studies, 8*(4), 539–549. https://doi.org/10.1080/14616700701411797

Bergmann, M. (1986). How many feminists does it take to make a joke? sexist humor and what's wrong with it. *Hypatia, 1*(1), 63–82. https://doi.org/10.1111/j.1527-2001.1986.tb00522.x

Bian, L., Leslie, S. J., & Cimpian, A. (2017). Gender stereotypes about intellectual ability emerge early and influence children's interests. *Science, 355*(6323), 389–391. https://doi.org/10.1126/SCIENCE.AAH6524

Bing, J. M. (2004). Is feminist humor an oxymoron? *Women and Language, 27*(1), 22–33.

Blackburn, R. E. (2018). *The performance of intersectionality on the 21st century stand-up comedy stage.* https://kuscholarworks.ku.edu/handle/1808/28057

Bore, I. L. K., & Reid, G. (2014). Laughing in the face of climate change? Satire as a device for engaging audiences in public debate. *Science Communication, 36*(4), 454–478. https://doi.org/10.1177/1075547014534076

Brake, M. (2019). *The science of The Big Bang Theory: What America's favorite sitcom can teach you about physics, flags, and the idiosyncrasies of scientists.* Skyhorse Publishing.

Brewer, & Ley, B. L. (2022). *Science in the media : popular images and public perceptions.* Routledge. https://www.routledge.com/Science-in-the-Media-Popular-Images-and-Public-Perceptions/Brewer-Ley/p/book/9781032033990?gclid=CjwKCAjw7p6aBhBiEiwA83fGutzEGrDSg0Z-AS6c1UJDnPBVIip653j-E_GeTDsF4RmCMcY1UiLOPxoC7-MQAvD_BwE

Buijzen, M., & Valkenburg, P. M. (2004). Developing a typology of humor in audiovisual media. *Media Psychology, 6*(2), 147–167. https://doi.org/10.1207/s1532785xmep0602_2

Carli, L. L., Alawa, L., Lee, Y., Zhao, B., & Kim, E. (2016). 'Stereotypes about gender and science: Women ≠ scientists. *Psychology of Women Quarterly, 40*(2), 244–260. https://doi.org/10.1177/0361684315622645

Ceci, S. J., & Williams, W. M. (2011). Understanding current causes of women's underrepresentation in science. *Proceedings of the National Academy of Sciences, 108*(8), 3157–3162. https://doi.org/10.1073/pnas.1014871108

Ceci, S. J., Ginther, D. K., Kahn, S., & Williams, W. M. (2014). Women in academic science: A changing landscape. *Psychological Science in the Public Interest, 15*(3), 75–141. https://doi.org/10.1177/1529100614541236

Charles, M. (2011). What gender is science? *Contexts, 10*(2), 22–28. https://doi.org/10.1177/1536504211408795

Cheryan, S., Master, A., & Meltzoff, A. N. (2015). Cultural stereotypes as gatekeepers: Increasing girls' interest in computer science and engineering by diversifying stereotypes. *Frontiers in Psychology, 49.* https://doi.org/10.3389/fpsyg.2015.00049

Cheryan, S., Ziegler, S. A., Montoya, A. K., & Jiang, L. (2017). Why are some STEM fields more gender balanced than others? *Psychological Bulletin, 143*(1), 1–35. https://doi.org/10.1037/bul0000052

Christensen, K. (1997). 'With whom do you believe your lot is cast?' White feminists and racism. *Signs: Journal of Women in Culture and Society, 22*(3), 617–648. https://doi.org/10.1086/495187

Clark, F., & Illman, D. L. (2006). A longitudinal study of the New York Times science times section. *Science Communication, 27*(4), 496–513. https://doi.org/10.1177/1075547006288010

Cole, K. K. (2015). "It's like she's eager to be verbally abused": Twitter, trolls, and (En)gendering disciplinary rhetoric. *Feminist Media Studies, 15*(2), 356–358. https://doi.org/10.1080/14680777.2015.1008750

Colpean, M., & Tully, M. (2019). Not just a joke: Tina Fey, Amy Schumer, and the weak reflexivity of white feminist comedy. *Women's Studies in Communication, 42*(2), 161–180. https://doi.org/10.1080/07491409.2019.161 0924

Cooper, K. M., Hendrix, T., Stephens, M. D., Cala, J. M., Mahrer, K., Krieg, A., Agloro, A. C. M., Badini, G. V., Barnes, M. E., Eledge, B., Jones, R., Lemon, E. C., Massimo, N. C., Martin, A., Ruberto, T., Simonson, K., Webb, E. A., Weaver, J., Zheng, Y., & Brownell, S. E. (2018). To be funny or not to be funny: Gender differences in student perceptions of instructor humor in college science courses. *PLoS ONE, 13*(8), e0201258–e0201258. https://doi.org/10.1371/journal.pone.0201258

Dawson, E., Archer, L., Seakins, A., Godec, S., DeWitt, J., King, H., Mau, A., & Nomikou, E. (2020). Selfies at the science museum: Exploring girls' identity performances in a science learning space. *Gender and Education, 32*(5), 664–681. https://doi.org/10.1080/09540253.2018.1557322

Dehdarirad, T., Villarroya, A., & Barrios, M. (2015). Research on women in science and higher education: A bibliometric analysis. *Scientometrics, 103*(3), 795–812. https://doi.org/10.1007/s11192-015-1574-x

Dickinson, P., Gilbert, J., Higgins, A., Matthew St. Pierre, P., Solomon, D., Zwagerman, S., Barreca, R., Bratton, J., Bush-Bailey, G., & Colletta, L. (2014). *Women and comedy: History, theory, practice.* Fairleigh Dickinson University Press.

Drakett, J., Rickett, B., Day, K., & Milnes, K. (2018). Old jokes, new media— Online sexism and constructions of gender in internet memes. *Feminism & Psychology, 28*(1), 109–127. https://doi.org/10.1177/0959353517727560

Eaton, A. A., Saunders, J. F., Jacobson, R. K., & West, K. (2020). How gender and race stereotypes impact the advancement of scholars in STEM: Professors' biased evaluations of physics and biology post-doctoral candidates. *Sex Roles, 82*(3), 127–141. https://doi.org/10.1007/s11199-019-01052-w

Eisend, M. (2009). A meta-analysis of humor in advertising. *Journal of the Academy of Marketing Science, 37*(2), 191–203. https://doi.org/10.1007/s11747-008-0096-y

Flicker, X. E., & Flicker, Eva". (2008). Women scientists in mainstream film: Social role models—Contribution to the public understanding of science from the perspective of film sociology. In P. Weingart & B. Hüppauf (Eds.), *Science Images and Popular Images of the Sciences,* (pp. 241–256). Routledge.

Fogg-Rogers, L. (2017). Does being human influence science and technology? *Journal of Science Communication, 16*(4), C04. https://doi.org/10.22323/2.16040304

Ford, T. E., Boxer, C. F., Armstrong, J., & Edel, J. R. (2008). More than "just a joke": The prejudice-releasing function of sexist humor. *Personality and Social Psychology Bulletin, 34*(2), 159–170. https://doi.org/10.1177/0146167207310022

Ford, T. E., Wentzel, E. R., & Lorion, J. (2001). Effects of exposure to sexist humor on perceptions of normative tolerance of sexism. *European Journal of Social Psychology, 31*(6), 677–691. https://doi.org/10.1002/ejsp.56

Ford, T. E., Woodzicka, J. A., Triplett, S. R., & Kochersberger, A. O. (2013). Sexist humor and beliefs that justify social sexism. *Current Research in Social Psychology, 21*(7), 64–81.

Francis, B., Archer, L., Moote, J., de Witt, J., & Yeomans, L. (2017). Femininity, science, and the denigration of the girly girl. *British Journal of Sociology of Education, 38*(8), 1097–1110. https://doi.org/10.1080/01425692.2016.1253455

Geena Davis Institute on Gender in Media. (2018). *The "Scully effect": I want to believe ... in STEM.* Geena Davis Institute on Gender in Media https://seejane.org/wp-content/uploads/x-files-scully-effect-report-geena-davis-institute.pdf

Gill, R. (2007). Postfeminist media culture: Elements of a sensibility. *European Journal of Cultural Studies, 10*(2), 147–166. https://doi.org/10.1177/1367549407075898

Gill, R. (2011). Sexism reloaded, or, it's time to get angry again! *Feminist Media Studies, 11*(1), 61–71. https://doi.org/10.1080/14680777.2011.537029

Gray, F. (1994). *Women and laughter.* Macmillan.

Greenwood, D., & Isbell, L. M. (2002). Ambivalent sexism and the dumb blonde: Men's and women's reactions to sexist jokes. *Psychology of Women Quarterly, 26*(4), 341–350. https://doi.org/10.1111/1471-6402.t01-2-00073

Griffin, M. (2022). "That moment meant a lot to my daughter": Affect, fandom, and Avengers: Endgame. *Feminist Media Studies,* 1–16. https://doi.org/10.1080/14680777.2022.2098801

Grugulis, I. (2002). Nothing serious? Candidates' use of humor in management training. *Human Relations, 55*(4), 387–406. https://doi.org/10.1177/0018726702055004459

Halpern, D. F., Benbow, C. P., Geary, D. C., Gur, R. C., Hyde, J. S., & Gernsbacher, M. A. (2007). The science of sex differences in science and mathematics. *Psychological Science in the Public Interest, 8*(1), 1–51. https://doi.org/10.1111/j.1529-1006.2007.00032.x

Hee, M., Jürgens, A.-S., Fiadotava, A., Judd, K., & Feldman, H. R. (2022). 'Communicating urgency through humor: School Strike 4 Climate protest placards'. *JCOM, 21*(05), A02. https://doi.org/10.22323/2.21050202

Hennefeld, M. (2017). Editor's introduction: Toward a feminist politics of comedy and history. *Feminist Media Histories, 3*(2), 1–14. https://doi.org/10.1525/fmh.2017.3.2.1

Holmes, C. (2017). *Laughing against white supremacy: Marginalized performance of resistance comedy.* Senior Independent Study Theses. Paper 7770. https://openworks.wooster.edu/independentstudy/7770

Hohenstein, S., & Thalmann, K. (2019). Difficult women: Changing representations of female characters in contemporary television series. *Zeitschrift Für Anglistik und Amerikanistik, 67*(2), 109–129. https://doi.org/10.1515/zaa-2019-0012

hooks, bell. (2014). "bell hooks' National Women's Studies Association Keynote Speech." National Women's Studies Association Conference, Nov. 14. http://www.nwsa.org/

Institute of Medicine. (2007). *Beyond bias and barriers: Fulfilling the potential of women in academic science and engineering.* The National Academies Press.https://doi.org/10.17226/11741

Johnston, J. C. (2014). Taking humour seriously: Women and the theatre of Virginie Ancelot. *Nottingham French Studies, 53*(3), 267–284. https://doi.org/10.3366/nfs.2014.0092

Judd, K., & McKinnon, M. (2021). A systematic map of inclusion, equity and diversity in science communication research: Do we practice what we preach? *Frontiers in Communication, 208.* https://doi.org/10.3389/fcomm.2021.744365

Jürgens, A.-S., Fiadotava, A., Tscharke, D. C., & Viaña, J. N. (2021). Spreading fun: Comic zombies, joker viruses and COVID-19 jokes. *Journal of Science & Popular Culture, 4*(1), 39–57. https://doi.org/10.1386/jspc_00024_1

Kaltenbacher, M., & Drews, S. (2020). An Inconvenient joke? A review of humor in climate change communication. *Environmental Communication, 14*(6), 717–729. https://doi.org/10.1080/17524032.2020.1756888

Kalviknes Bore, I.-L. (2010). (Un)funny women: TV comedy audiences and the gendering of humour. *European Journal of Cultural Studies., 13*(2), 139–154. https://doi.org/10.1177/1367549409352272

Kelly, A. (1985). The construction of masculine science. *British Journal of Sociology of Education, 6*(2), 133–154. https://doi.org/10.1080/0142569850060201

Knobloch-Westerwick, S., Glynn, C. J., & Huge, M. (2013). The Matilda Effect in science communication: An experiment on gender bias in publication quality perceptions and collaboration interest. *Science Communication, 35*(5), 603–625. https://doi.org/10.1177/1075547012472684

Kobayashi, S., & Berge, M. (2022). Learning norms of science through laughter: A study of humour in life science supervision. *International Journal of Science Education, 44*(10), 1680–1699. https://doi.org/10.1080/09500693.2022. 2090634

Kuchynka, S. L., Salomon, K., Bosson, J. K., El-Hout, M., Kiebel, E., Cooperman, C., & Toomey, R. (2018). Hostile and benevolent sexism and college women's STEM outcomes. *Psychology of Women Quarterly, 42*(1), 72–87. https://doi.org/10.1177/0361684317741889

Kuipers, G. (2006). *Good humor, bad taste: A sociology of the joke* (Vol. 7). De Gruyter Mouton. https://doi.org/10.1515/9783110898996

LaFollette, M. C. (1988). Eyes on the stars: Images of women scientists in popular magazines. *Science, Technology, & Human Values, 13*(3–4), 262–275. https://doi.org/10.1177/016224398801303-407

Lauzen, M., Dozier, D., & Horan, N. (2008). Constructing gender stereotypes through social roles in prime-time television. *Journal of Broadcasting & Electronic Media, 52*, 200–214. https://doi.org/10.1080/088381508019 91971

Lewenstein, B. (2019). The need for feminist approaches to science communication. *Journal of Science Communication, 18*(04), C01. https://doi.org/10. 22323/2.18040301

Li, P. R. (2016). *Communicating science through entertainment television: How the sitcom The Big Bang Theory influences audience perceptions of science and scientists.* [PhD Thesis] The Australian National University. https://doi.org/ 10.25911/5d78d671bc21c

Lockyer, S. (2020). Women and comedy. In K. Ross, I. Bachmann, V. Cardo, S. Moorti & M. Scarcelli (Eds.), *The International Encyclopedia of Gender, Media, and Communication*, (pp. 1–7). Wiley. https://doi.org/10.1002/978 1119429128.iegmc237

Lockyer, S., & Pickering, M. (2008). You must be joking: The sociological critique of humour and comic media. *Sociology Compass, 2*(3), 808–820. https://doi.org/10.1111/j.1751-9020.2008.00108.x

Long, M., Steinke, J., Applegate, B., Knight Lapinski, M., Johnson, M. J., & Ghosh, S. (2010). Portrayals of male and female scientists in television programs popular among middle school-age children. *Science Communication, 32*(3), 356–382. https://doi.org/10.1177/1075547009357779

Ma, Z., & Jiang, M. (2013). Interpretation of verbal humor in the sitcom The Big Bang Theory from the perspective of adaptation-relevance theory. *Theory*

and Practice in Language Studies, 3(12), 2220–2226. https://doi.org/10.
4304/tpls.3.12.2220-2226

Mackie, M. (1990). Who is laughing now?: The role of humour in the social construction of gender. *Atlantis: Critical Studies in Gender, Culture & Social Justice, 15*(2), 11–26. https://journals.msvu.ca/index.php/atlantis/article/view/4247

Mallett, R. K., Ford, T. E., & Woodzicka, J. A. (2016). What did he mean by that? Humor Decreases attributions of sexism and confrontation of sexist jokes. *Sex Roles, 75*(5), 272–284. https://doi.org/10.1007/s11199-016-0605-2

McIntosh, H. (2014). Representations of female scientists in The Big Bang Theory. *Journal of Popular Film and Television, 42*(4), 195–204. https://doi.org/10.1080/01956051.2014.896779

McKinnon, M., & O'Connell, C. (2020). Perceptions of stereotypes applied to women who publicly communicate their STEM work. *Humanities and Social Sciences Communications, 7*, 160. https://doi.org/10.1057/s41599-020-00654-0

Medin, D. L., & Bang, M. (2014). The cultural side of science communication. *Proceedings of the National Academy of Sciences, 111*(Supplement 4), 13621–13626. https://doi.org/10.1073/pnas.1317510111

Meyer, J. C. (2000). Humor as a double-edged sword: Four functions of humor in communication. *Communication Theory, 10*(3), 310–331. https://doi.org/10.1111/j.1468-2885.2000.tb00194.x

Miller, D. I., Eagly, A. H., & Linn, M. C. (2015). Women's representation in science predicts national gender-science stereotypes: Evidence from 66 nations. *Journal of Educational Psychology, 107*(3), 631–644. https://doi.org/10.1037/edu0000005

Miner, K. N., Walker, J. M., Bergman, M. E., Jean, V. A., Carter-Sowell, A., January, S. C., & Kaunas, C. (2018). From "her" problem to "our" problem: Using an individual lens versus a social-structural lens to understand gender inequity in STEM. *Industrial and Organizational Psychology, 11*(2), 267–290. https://doi.org/10.1017/iop.2018.7

Mitchell, M., & McKinnon, M. (2019). 'Human' or 'objective' faces of science? Gender stereotypes and the representation of scientists in the media. *Public Understanding of Science, 28*(2), 177–190. https://doi.org/10.1177/0963662518801257

Mizejewski, L., & Sturtevant, V. (Eds.). (2017). *Hysterical!: Women in American comedy.* University of Texas Press. https://doi.org/10.7560/314517

Morreall, J. (2016). Philosophy of humor. In E.N. Zalta (Ed.), *Stanford encyclopedia of philosophy* Stanford University. https://plato.stanford.edu/entries/humor/

Mostafa, T. (2019). Why don't more girls choose to pursue a science career? *PISA in Focus*, No. 93, OECD Publishing. https://doi.org/10.1787/02b d2b68-en

National Science Board. (2022). *Science and engineering indicators 2022.* The State of U.S. Science and Engineering. NSB-2022–1. Alexandria, VA: National Science Foundation. https://ncses.nsf.gov/pubs/nsb20221

National Science Board. (2024). *Science and engineering indicators 2024.* The State of U.S. Science and Engineering. NSB-2024–3. Alexandria, VA: National Science Foundation. https://ncses.nsf.gov/pubs/nsb20243

Nelson, D. J., & Cheng, H. N. (2018). Diversity in Science: An overview. In D. J. Nelson & H.N. Cheng (Eds.) *Diversity in the scientific community volume 1: Quantifying diversity and formulating success* (pp. 1–12). ACS Symposium Series 1255.

O'Brien, L. T., Blodorn, A., Adams, G., Garcia, D. M., & Hammer, E. (2015). Ethnic variation in gender-STEM stereotypes and STEM participation: An intersectional approach. *Cultural Diversity and Ethnic Minority Psychology, 21*(2), 169. https://doi.org/10.1037/a0037944

O'Connell, C., & McKinnon, M. (2021). Perceptions of barriers to career progression for academic women in STEM. *Societies, 11*(2), 27. https://doi.org/10.3390/soc11020027

O'Neill, S., & Nicholson-Cole, S. (2009). "Fear won't do it" promoting positive engagement with climate change through visual and iconic representations. *Science Communication, 30*(3), 355–379. https://doi.org/10.1177/107554 7008329201

Osborne, A. (2023). *Trans joy: Examining and developing intersectional trans women in narrative comedy* [Master's Thesis, Queensland University of Technology]. https://eprints.qut.edu.au/238192/

Osnes, B., Boykoff, M., & Chandler, P. (2019). Good-natured comedy to enrich climate communication. *Comedy Studies, 10*(2), 224–236. https://doi.org/ 10.1080/2040610X.2019.1623513

Parker, P. D., Van Zanden, B., & Parker, R. B. (2018). Girls get smart, boys get smug: Historical changes in gender differences in math, literacy, and academic social comparison and achievement. *Learning and Instruction, 54*, 125–137. https://doi.org/10.1016/j.learninstruc.2017.09.002

Pickering, M., & Lockyer, S. (2005). Introduction: The ethics and aesthetics of humour and comedy. In S. Lockyer & M. Pickering (Eds.), *Beyond a joke: The limits of humour* (pp. 1–24). Palgrave Macmillan.

Pietri, E. S., Johnson, I. R., Majid, S., & Chu, C. (2021). Seeing what's possible: videos are more effective than written portrayals for enhancing the relatability of scientists and promoting black female students' interest in STEM. *Sex Roles, 84*(1–2), 14–33. https://doi.org/10.1007/s11199-020-01153-x

Pinto, B., Marçal, D., & Vaz, S. G. (2015). Communicating through humour. A project of stand-up comedy about science. *Public Understanding of Science, 24*(7), 776–793. https://doi.org/10.1177/0963662513511175

Pinto, B., & Riesch, H. (2017). Are audiences receptive to humour in popular science articles? An exploratory study using articles on environmental issues. *Journal of Science Communication, 16*(4), A01, 1–15. https://doi.org/10.22323/2.16040201

Powell, K. (2022). Female scientists can advance by saying: 'Yes, I'll do it'. *Nature, 602*(7898), 711–712. https://doi.org/10.1038/d41586-022-00377-z

Pramita, A. (2021). Language and humor in The Big Bang Theory. *ENLIT Journal, 1*(2), 65–76. https://doi.org/10.33654/enlit.v1i2.1384

Price, J., & Payne. A. M. (2019). *2019 Women for media report: 'You Can't Be what you can't see.'* https://media.ourwatch.org.au/resource/2019-women-for-media-report-you-cant-be-what-you-cant-see/

Quart, A. (2012, October 30). The age of hipster sexism. *The Cut.* https://www.thecut.com/2012/10/age-of-hipster-sexism.html

Rasekoala, E. (2019). The seeming paradox of the need for a feminist agenda for science communication and the notion of science communication as a 'ghetto' of women's over-representation: Perspectives, interrogations and nuances from the global south. *Journal of Science Communication, 18*(04), C07. https://doi.org/10.22323/2.18040307

Rhodes, N., & Ellithorpe, M. E. (2016). Laughing at risk: Sitcom laugh tracks communicate norms for behavior. *Media Psychology, 19*(3), 359–380. https://doi.org/10.1080/15213269.2015.1090908

Riesch, H. (2015). Why did the proton cross the road? Humour and science communication. *Public Understanding of Science, 24*(7), 768–775. https://doi.org/10.1177/0963662514546299

Riquelme, A. R., Carretero-Dios, H., Megías, J. L., & Romero-Sánchez, M. (2021). Joking for gender equality: Subversive humor against sexism motivates collective action in men and women with weaker feminist identity. *Sex Roles, 84*(1), 1–13. https://doi.org/10.1007/s11199-020-01154-w

Riquelme, A. R., Carretero-Dios, H., Megías, J. L., & Romero-Sánchez, M. (2023). Subversive humor against sexism: Conceptualization and first evidence on its empirical nature. *Current Psychology, 42*(19), 16208–16221. https://doi.org/10.1007/s12144-019-00331-9

Rodrigues, L., Takahashi, B., Tiffany, L. A., Menezes, S., & Valdéz-Ward, E. (2023). Minoritized scientists in the United States: an identity perspective to science communication. *Science Communication, 45*(5), 567–595. https://doi.org/10.1177/10755470231199955

Rosser, S. V. (2018). Breaking into the lab: Engineering progress for women in science and technology. *International Journal of Gender, Science and Technology, 10*(2), 213–232. https://genderandset.open.ac.uk/index.php/gender andset/article/view/490

Rowe, K. (1995). *The unruly woman : Gender and the genres of laughter.* University of Texas Press.

Santos, D., & Jürgens, A.-S. (2023). From Harleen Quinzel to Harley Quinn: Science, symmetry and transformation. *Journal of Graphic Novels & Comics, 15*(2), 283–297.

Sartika, L. A., & Pranoto, B. E. (2021). Analysis of humor in The Big Bang Theory by using relevance theory: A pragmatic study. *Linguistics and Literature Journal, 2*(1), 1–7. https://doi.org/10.33365/llj.v2i1.292

Sassler, S., Glass, J., Levitte, Y., & Michelmore, K. M. (2017). The missing women in STEM? Assessing gender differentials in the factors associated with transition to first jobs. *Social Science Research, 63*, 192–208. https://doi.org/10.1016/j.ssresearch.2016.09.014

Saucier, D. A., Strain, M. L., Miller, S. S., O'Dea, C. J., & Till, D. F. (2018). "What do you call a Black guy who flies a plane?": The effects and understanding of disparagement and confrontational racial humor. *Humor, 31*(1), 105–128. https://doi.org/10.1515/humor-2017-0107

Scheufele, D. A. (2013). Communicating science in social settings. *Proceedings of the National Academy of Sciences, 110*(3), 14040–14047. https://doi.org/10.1073/pnas.1213275110

Shachar, O. (2000). Spotlighting women scientists in the press: Tokenism in science journalism. *Public Understanding of Science, 9*(4), 347–358. https://doi.org/10.1088/0963-6625/9/4/301

Shifman, L., & Lemish, D. (2011). "Mars and Venus" in virtual space: Postfeminist humor and the internet. *Critical Studies in Media Communication, 28*(3), 253–273. https://doi.org/10.1080/15295036.2010.522589

Shifman, L., & Lemish, D. (2010). Between feminism and fun(ny)mism: Analysing gender in popular internet humour. *Information, Communication & Society, 13*(6), 870–891. https://doi.org/10.1080/136911809034 90560

Sikora, J. (2019). Is it all about early occupational expectations? How the gender gap in two science domains reproduces itself at subsequent stages of education: Evidence from longitudinal PISA in Australia. *International Journal of Science Education, 41*(16), 2347–2368. https://doi.org/10.1080/09500693.2019.1676933

Simis, M. J., Yeo, S. K., Rose, K. M., Brossard, D., Scheufele, D. A., Xenos, M. A., & Pope, B. K. (2015). New media audiences' perceptions of male and female scientists in two sci-fi movies. *Bulletin of Science, Technology & Society, 35*(3–4), 93–103. https://doi.org/10.1177/0270467616636195

Skurka, C., Niederdeppe, J., & Nabi, R. (2019). Kimmel on climate: Disentangling the emotional ingredients of a satirical monologue. *Science Communication*, *41*(4), 394–421. https://doi.org/10.1177/1075547019853837

Skurka, C., Niederdeppe, J., Romero-Canyas, R., & Acup, D. (2018). Pathways of influence in emotional appeals: Benefits and tradeoffs of using fear or humor to promote climate change-related intentions and risk perceptions. *Journal of Communication*, *68*(1), 169–193. https://doi.org/10.1093/joc/jqx008

Smith, C. (2022). bell hooks (1952–2021). *History in the Making*, *15*(11), 205–228. https://scholarworks.lib.csusb.edu/history-in-the-making/vol15/iss1/11

Soucy-Humphreys, J., Judd, K., & Jürgens, A.-S. (2023). Challenging the stereotype through humor? Comic female scientists in animated TV series for young audiences. *Frontiers in Communication*, *7*, 1024602. https://doi.org/10.3389/fcomm.2022.1024602

Sperber, D., & Wilson, D. (1995). *Relevance: Communication and cognition*. Wiley-Blackwell.

Starr, C. R. (2018). I'm Not a Science Nerd! *Psychology of Women Quarterly*, *42*(4), 489–503. https://doi.org/10.1177/0361684318793848

Steele, C. M. (1997). A threat in the air: How stereotypes shape intellectual identity and performance. *American Psychologist*, *52*(6), 613–629. https://doi.org/10.1037/0003-066X.52.6.613

Steinke, J. (1997). A portrait of a woman as a scientist: Breaking down barriers created by gender-role stereotypes. *Public Understanding of Science*, *6*(4), 409–428. https://doi.org/10.1088/0963-6625/6/4/006

Steinke, J. (2005). Cultural representations of gender and science: Portrayals of female scientists and engineers in popular films. *Science Communication*, *27*(1), 27–63. https://doi.org/10.1177/1075547005278610

Steinke, J. (2012). Portrayals of female scientists in the mass media. In A. N. Valdivia (Ed.), *The International Encyclopedia of Media Studies*. Wiley. https://doi.org/10.1002/9781444361506.wbiems070

Steinke, J. (2017). Adolescent girls' STEM identity formation and media images of STEM professionals: Considering the influence of contextual cues. *Frontiers in Psychology*, *8*, 1–15. https://doi.org/10.3389/fpsyg.2017.00716

Sunderland, J. (2007). Contradictions in gendered discourses: Feminist readings of sexist jokes? *Gender and Language*, *1*(2), 207–228. https://doi.org/10.1558/genl.v1i2.207

Thébaud, S., & Charles, M. (2018). Segregation, stereotypes, and STEM. *Social Sciences*, *7*(7), 1–19. https://doi.org/10.3390/socsci7070111

Tuchman, G. (2000). The symbolic annihilation of women by the mass media. In L. Crothers & C. Lockhart (Eds.), *Culture and politics: A Reader* (pp. 150–174). Palgrave Macmillan. https://doi.org/10.1007/978-1-349-62397-6_9

United Nations Department of Economic and Social Affairs. (2023). *The sustainable development goals report 2023: Special edition.* United Nations. https://doi.org/10.18356/9789210024914

van Veelen, R., Derks, B., & Endedijk, M. D. (2019). Double trouble: How being outnumbered and negatively stereotyped threatens career outcomes of women in STEM. *Frontiers in Psychology, 10*(150). https://doi.org/10.3389/fpsyg.2019.00150

Weber, L. (2017). *'Don't be such a girl, I'm only joking!' post-alternative comedy, British panel shows, and masculine spaces* [Master's Thesis, The University of Wisconsin—Milwaukee]. https://www.proquest.com/docview/1966703886/abstract/E68445AEB3254C59PQ/1

White, R. (2018). *Television comedy and femininity: Queering gender.* Bloomsbury Publishing. https://www.bloomsbury.com/uk/television-comedy-and-femininity-9781784533625/

Woodzicka, J. A., & Ford, T. E. (2010). A framework for thinking about the (not-so-funny) effects of sexist humor. *Europe's Journal of Psychology, 6*(3), Article 3. https://doi.org/10.5964/ejop.v6i3.217

Worth, A., Augoustinos, M., & Hastie, B. (2016). "Playing the gender card": Media representations of Julia Gillard's sexism and misogyny speech. *Feminism & Psychology, 26*(1), 52–72. https://doi.org/10.1177/0959353515605544

Yeo, S. K., Su, L.Y.-F., Cacciatore, M. A., McKasy, M., & Qian, S. (2020). Predicting intentions to engage with scientific messages on twitter: The roles of mirth and need for humor. *Science Communication, 42*(4), 481–507. https://doi.org/10.1177/1075547020942512

Yıldırım, B., Öcal, E., & Şahin-Topalcengiz, E. (2021). STEM in movies: Female preservice teachers' perspectives on movie "Hidden Figures". *Journal of Baltic Science Education, 20*(5), 740–758. https://doi.org/10.33225/jbse/21.20.740

Yong, E. (2018, February 7). I spent two years trying to fix the gender imbalance in my stories. *The Atlantic.* https://www.theatlantic.com/science/archive/2018/02/i-spent-two-years-trying-to-fix-the-gender-imbalance-in-my-stories/552404/

Yongping, R. (2004). Adaptation-Relevance analysis in verbal communication. *Foreign Languages Research, 117*, 28–33.

Zobel, D. (2015). *The science of TV'S big bang theory: Explanations even Penny would understand.* ECW Press.

CHAPTER 3

"I Thought You'd Be Doing Each Other's Nails and Buying Matching Tote Bags off Etsy": Theoretical Frameworks and Methods

Abstract This chapter of *Women Scientists in American Television Comedy: Beakers, Big Bangs and Broken Hearts* focuses on the theoretical frameworks and methods used to analyze the portrayal of women scientists in TV comedies. The study draws on Eva Flicker's model of seven women scientist stereotypes and Jocelyn Steinke's frameworks for analyzing women scientists in media. It adapts these models to understand the use of humor in depicting women scientists in TV shows like *Never Have I Ever*, *The Big Bang Theory* and *Zoey's Extraordinary Playlist*. The chapter also utilizes Moniek Buijzen and Patti M. Valkenburg's typology of humor, identifying humor types such as slapstick, irony and satire in these shows. The research involved a qualitative textual analysis of 47 episodes, examining how humor shapes cultural ideas about women in STEM. The sample TV shows were selected based on their commercial success and portrayal of women scientists. The chapter outlines the process of identifying and analyzing humor types and their impact on the portrayal of women scientists, aiming to understand how these portrayals influence public perceptions and cultural stereotypes. The findings highlight the complexity and nuance of humorous representations of women in STEM fields.

© The Author(s), under exclusive license to Springer Nature   43
Switzerland AG 2025
K. Judd et al., *Women Scientists in American Television Comedy*,
Palgrave Studies in Science and Popular Culture,
https://doi.org/10.1007/978-3-031-81525-6_3

Keywords Humor typology · Textual analysis · Women scientist stereotypes

The study presented in *Women Scientists in American Television Comedy: Beakers, Big Bangs and Broken Hearts* used a combination of interpretive frameworks and methods to investigate the relationship between the use of humor and the representation of women scientists in American television comedies. While our methods did not include "doing each other's nails and buying matching tote bags off Etsy" (*Zoey's Extraordinary Playlist S01E1*) as a male colleague in one of the shows characterized the STEM work of women, we did use textual analysis informed by frameworks developed by Flicker (2008), Steinke (2005, 2017) and Buijzen and Valkenburg (2004).

INTERPRETIVE FRAMEWORK: WOMEN SCIENTIST STEREOTYPES

A number of key theoretical frameworks informed both our analysis and interpretation of the selected 47 TV episodes of the TV comedies *Never Have I Ever*, *The Big Bang Theory* and *Zoey's Extraordinary Playlist*. First, our study draws on Eva Flicker's (2008) seminal model of seven women scientist stereotypes in popular film: the old maid, the gruff women's libber, the naïve expert, the evil vamp, the daughter or assistant, the lonely heroine and the clever, digital beauty. Interpretations of 60 feature films were used by Flicker to classify women scientist characters into these categories based on the three dimensions of social status (e.g., profession, qualification, hierarchy, team decisions), social relations (e.g., professional/private; functional/emotional social role models) and attributive gender qualities (e.g., bodily traits, qualities, character, clothing, language) (Flicker, 2008, p. 246). Studies of the portrayal of women scientists in film continue to base analysis on Flicker's (2008) descriptions of these stereotypes (see Deater, 2021; Kool et al., 2022; Sagatov, 2019) and we follow their lead. In particular, we draw on Flicker's (2008) stereotypes to better understand if women scientists in contemporary comedy TV shows comply with or challenge stereotypes established in our cultural representation.

Our approach also builds on Jocelyn Steinke's frameworks for analyzing women scientists in film and television (Steinke, 2005, 2017; Steinke & Paniagua Talvarez, 2017). Steinke's textual analyses use a priori codes relating to the themes of physical appearance, romantic relationships, expertise, competency, work-life balance and parental status (Steinke, 2005; Steinke & Paniagua Talvarez, 2017). Analysis of films from 1991 to 2001 suggests that depictions of women scientists present them in positions of high professional status while emphasizing ideas of appearance and romance, and reinforcing traditional social and cultural assumptions about the role of women in STEM (Steinke, 2005). Against the background of our specific sample television series, Steinke's research (2005, 2017) helped us develop our core themes of this study—occupation and stereotypes—which brings new facets to the discussion, as Steinke did not focus on television comedies.

Both Steinke's (2005) findings and Flicker's (2008) sociological interpretive framework and women scientist typology were used by Kool et al. (2022) to examine how women scientists were portrayed in contemporary films from 2013 to 2020 in the context of fourth-wave feminism. To guide their analysis, Kool et al. (2022) use interpretation questions to understand the occupational portrayal of women scientists as well as the socio-political and temporal contexts that the characters existed in. Like Kool et al. (2022), we also engage in a sociological film interpretation of contemporary TV shows to understand the portrayal of women scientists and their stereotypes—albeit specifically in the context of humor—and adopt their interpretation questions as a useful structural tool for our analysis. In addition to this framework of women scientist stereotypes, we also intentionally considered intersectionality throughout our interpretations to develop more nuanced understanding of the characters in our study.

Intersectionality, a term coined by Kimberlé Crenshaw (1989) to understand the compounding and dynamic implications of identity on power, privilege and relationships has expanded over the decades since (Hill Collins & Bilge, 2016) to become an established critical framework well beyond its academic law origins (Cho et al., 2013; Grzanka, 2020). Cooper (2015) argues that the aim of intersectional analysis is not to fully understand an individual through their various identities, but to make them 'knowable' within the complex fabric of society. Intersectionality seeks to reveal the hidden effects of societal structures on individuals, taking into account their whole selves, rather than a single facet such as sex, race, class or sexuality (Hill Collins & Bilge, 2016). This is the case not only in terms of oppressions, but also privileges—many people will have a combination of both, as well as aspects of their identity that are not clearly one or the other (Crenshaw, 1989). While intersectionality influenced the interpretations of the present study, it was not used explicitly as an interpretive framework itself. In sum, we adapt Steinke's (2005, 2017) themes of women scientists in film and incorporate Flicker's women scientist stereotypes to create interpretation questions, inspired by Kool et al. (2022), to guide our analysis of the use of humor in portraying these themes. Drawing upon these interpretive contexts, we aim to understand if, and what, humor is used in scenes portraying women scientists and how this portrayal contributes to cultural ideas of women in STEM.

Interpretive Framework: Humor Typology

Against the background of major humor theories (see Chapter 2), Buijzen and Valkenburg (2004) analyzed the content of 319 humorous television commercials to investigate whether and how humor types are grouped into higher-order humor categories, and which humor types and categories exactly characterize these commercials (aimed at different audience groups). They identified 41 humor types which they combined into seven broader categories: slapstick, clownish humor, surprise, misunderstanding, irony, satire and parody. The study identified that commercials aimed at children and adolescents most commonly used slapstick humor, while slapstick, ironic and satirical humor dominated those aimed at men and surprise, slapstick and ironic humor were most frequently employed in commercials aimed at women (Buijzen & Valkenburg, 2004, pp. 157–161). Our own humor analysis is guided by their approach. Although published in 2004, this typology continues to be a useful approach (see Su et al., 2022)—also taking into account different humor theories and showing that many humor types are not necessarily inherently funny: "they must complement one another to generate humor" (Buijzen & Valkenburg, 2004, p. 149). To adapt both their typology and inductive approach to humor to the medium of television shows, we first reviewed the episodes and scenes featuring women scientists in our sample to identify the humor types associated with the women scientists and then conducted an analysis and interpretation of the many ways in which they shape their portrayal. The humor types identified in sequences relating to

Table 3.1 Humor types identified in episodes relating to women scientist characters in the sample

Humor type	Short description
Absurdity	Nonsense and ridiculous, a situation that goes against all logical rules or silly in a humorous way
Dark	Grim or depressing humor dealing with taboo or vulgar issues
Deadpan	Lacking expression with an impassive and matter-of-fact presentation
Exaggeration	Making an exaggeration or overstatement; reacting in an exaggerated way; exaggerating the qualities of a person or product
Farce	Improbable and exaggerated situations with satirical elements
Irony	Expression of one thing but has meaning of exactly the opposite
Mordant	Caustic criticism or mocking of someone or something
Ridicule	Making a fool of someone, verbally or nonverbally
Sarcasm	Biting remark made with a hostile tone; sarcasm is always a verbal put down
Satire	Using humor to expose or criticize well-known things, situations, public figures or topical issues
Schadenfreude	Experiencing pleasure or self-satisfaction when learning of or witnessing the troubles, failures or humiliation of another
Self-deprecating	Humor where the communicator targets themselves for comedic effect
Sexual allusion	Making a reference or insinuation to sexual matters
Stereotype	Stereotyped or generalized way of depicting members of a certain nation, gender or other group

Humor type definitions were adapted from Buijzen and Valkenburg (2004) typology of humor in audiovisual media

the women scientist(s) from the sample episodes, and their definitions, are listed in Table 3.1.

TELEVISION PROGRAM SAMPLE

The sample consisted of commercially successful television series categorized as a 'comedy' on the Internet Movie Database (IMDb) that featured one or more women working in a STEM field. We identified these programs using purposive internet-based research of website pages mentioning TV series featuring women in STEM. Based on these criteria, three TV series were selected: *Never Have I Ever*, *The Big Bang Theory* and *Zoey's Extraordinary Playlist*.

Never Have I Ever (2020–2023) is an American coming-of-age comedy-drama, created by Mindy Kaling and Lang Fisher. The series follows the daily life of an Indian-American high school student, Devi Vishwakumar after the sudden death of her father. The series features one woman scientist character, Kamala, who is Devi's older cousin and a biology Ph.D. student at Caltech in Pasadena, California. In Season 2 of the series, Kamala is shown working in a male-dominated laboratory, where she struggles to receive recognition for her work and respect from her colleagues (for more details see *Never Have I Ever* on IMDb).

The Big Bang Theory (2017–2019) is one of the most popular American sitcoms of all time, broadcasting 279 episodes over 12 seasons. The science-themed series was produced by Chuck Lorre and Bill Prady, along with the executive producer, Steven Molaro. The series follows the humorous events of a group of four friends and colleagues working at Caltech in Pasadena, California: Sheldon Cooper, a theoretical physicist, Leonard Hofstadter, an experimental physicist, Howard Wolowitz, an aerospace engineer, and Rajesh Koothrappali, a particle astrophysicist. Contrasting the scientists is Leonard and Sheldon's neighbor, Penny, a waitress and aspiring actress from Nebraska. In Season 3, two recurring women scientists are introduced as love interests for the main characters. First is Bernadette Rostenkowski, a microbiology student who later earns her Ph.D. and a high-paying job in a pharmaceutical company. Bernadette develops a relationship with Howard who she later marries and starts a family. Second is Amy Farrah Fowler, a neurobiologist, selected as a potential partner for Sheldon on an online dating site due to their shared intellect (for more details see *The Big Bang Theory* on IMDb).

Zoey's Extraordinary Playlist (2020–2021) is an American musical comedy-drama, created by Austin Winsberg. The series follows the life of a young software developer, Zoey Clarke, who – after a freak accident in an MRI machine – develops the ability to hear people's innermost thoughts as large musical numbers. The series features two women software engineers: Zoey, who first becomes the manager of an all-male team at her tech firm and then later is promoted to the executive director; and Joan, who is initially the executive director of the team. As a musical-comedy, humor is a core element of the construction of *Zoey's Extraordinary Playlist*. The series features elaborate and often humorous musical numbers, which are figments of Zoey's imagination (for more detail see *Zoey's Extraordinary Playlist* on IMBd).

What all three TV series have in common is that they have had significant commercial success. The fourth and final season of *Never Have I Ever* debuted in the No. 1 position on Netflix's weekly viewership

Table 3.2 Keywords used for inclusion of episodes in the sample

	TV Show		
	Never Have I Ever	The Big Bang Theory	Zoey's Extraordinary Playlist
Woman Scientist Character	Kamala	Amy; Bernadette	Zoey; Joan
Science-related keyword	Article; Lab; Laboratory; Research; Science; Scientist; Work; Working	Experiment; Lab; Laboratory; PhD; Project; Research; Science; Scientific; Thesis	Engineer; Engineering; Project; Software; SPRQ; SPRQ Point; Work; Working; Workplace

charts, with 11.5 million views over its debut week (Hailu, 2023). From Season 6 through 11, the viewership of *The Big Bang Theory* averaged 18 million viewers (Fitzgerald, 2019). The Season 2 debut of *Zoey's Extraordinary Playlist* averaged approximately 3 million viewers, a 10% increase in viewers from the previous season (Otterson, 2021). These popular and internationally successful television series are part of the contemporary media culture in the United States from which they originate, but as American media culture is increasingly present throughout the world, we follow Douglas Kellner in considering them of "global and not merely regional interest" (2020, p. 9). Due to the limited number of contemporary comedy television programs featuring women scientists in a lead or supporting role, a purposive sample was used. To compile television episodes for analysis, episode synopses on Wikipedia were screened for keywords to yield episodes relating to the women scientists working or discussing science. Episodes were included in the sample if the synopsis included the name of at least one woman scientist character and at least one science-related keyword pertinent to each series (see Table 3.2). As a result of these criteria, a total of 47 episodes were included in the sample.

Textual Analysis

The purpose of this research—undertaken by researchers from the fields of Science Communication and Cultural Studies who specialize in the intersections between science and humor in pop culture, and in equity and diversity in STEM contexts—was to explore the types of humor that characterize portrayals of women scientists, and how this humor is used to shape cultural ideas of (the reality of) women in STEM. To gain insight into the TV representation of the lived experiences of women scientists and how this may be interpreted and internalized by audiences, a qualitative textual analysis of 47 episodes was conducted. Textual analysis is a common approach in film/media analysis used to understand processes of sense- and meaning-making across different cultural mediums—or, in other words, texts (a text is something we make meaning from, see, e.g., Larson, 1991; McKee, 2003). Although textual analysis is widely used, it has only recently attracted more explicit attention in the context of science communication and science-in-pop-culture studies (e.g. Jürgens et al., 2024; Thompson et al., 2023). Textual analysis helps to clarify how factors of influence can be detected (e.g. the influence of a particular context or medium on the development of a theme); how thought structures and motif patterns can be produced; knowledge and attitudes can unfold; unintended and unexpected connections investigated and ultimately new perspectives created and gained. As explained by Jürgens et al. (2024, p. 11): "Overall, studying science in culture—via textual analysis—matters because it can advance society's knowledge about the cultural power and human experience of science". Jensen (1991, p. 4) describes qualitative textual analysis as an approach that can "examine meaning production as a *process* which is contextualized and inextricably integrated with wider social and cultural practices". Therefore, analysis of the manifest and latent content of comedic TV episodes can provide insight into the dominant values and stereotypes of women scientists in society.

The framework for qualitative thematic analysis was based on previous studies of dominant themes and stereotypes used in portraying women scientists in television and film (Flicker, 2008; Steinke, 2005, 2017). Based on these insights from the research, two core themes were developed—occupation and stereotype—from which interpretation questions were created following Kool et al.'s (2022) method for sociological film analysis (see above). The interpretation questions (Table 3.3) used were modified to fit the purpose of this study to understand how humor is used when representing commonly depicted aspects of women scientists in TV. A description of different audiovisual segments that apply to each theme-based interpretation question is provided below (Table 3.3). For each of the interpretation questions, we used the typology of humor in

audiovisual media developed by Buijzen and Valkenburg (2004) to identify the *specific* humor types employed in scenes relevant to our core
themes within the context of other relevant communicative techniques,
such as dialogue, character behavior, setting/environment, costumes,
videography and editing.

We then analyzed and interpreted the sample using a qualitative
deductive approach guided by the interpretation questions, as we were
interested in meaning, processes of sense-making, how structures of
thoughts and patterns are presented through distinctive forms of humor
and how specific characteristics create meaning or contrast each other
(Creswell, 2014, p. 4). Our analysis focused on scenes relevant to the
interpretation questions where humor was present—identified by one
author either through the use of a laugh track or through recognizing
the humor types of Buijzen and Valkenburg's (2004) typology. A subset
of n = 20 episodes was reviewed by a second author to confirm the scenes
used in analysis and the humor types identified within. Each episode in
the sample was viewed twice by the coder, who took contemporaneous
film notes on: the humor styles and type used in a scene; the context, *mise
en scène* and relevant dialogue; and the portrayal of women scientists in
the context of our interpretation questions. An example of the film notes
is as follows:

> Sheldon enters Leonard and Penny's apartment and tells them "I've been
> enjoying my collaboration with Amy but ever since we got back from our
> honeymoon, she has so little time." Leonard replies "Well, she does have
> her own job" to which Sheldon replies "Yeah, but it's so dull" and then
> mocks Amy's research, saying in a sarcastic tone "trying to understand
> how the brain translates the five senses into biochemical information. I'd
> rather wait in line without my phone". This is followed by a laugh track.
> Sheldon is then shown approaching Amy's superior and asks him to have
> Amy's project reassigned to someone else so he and Amy can work on
> Sheldon's 'String Theory' work instead. Sheldon assures Amy's superior in
> a deadpan, matter-of-fact manner, that they will not engage in any sexual
> relations given they are newlyweds, saying:"Let me assure you, we will not
> engage in workplace coitus" which is followed by a laugh track.

After data collection was complete, recurring patterns in the use of humor
against Steinke's (2005, 2017) themes of women scientists and Flicker's (2008) stereotype model were compared across the three TV series
and presented in the findings chapter in the next section. As we will
see in the following chapters, analyzing key episodes of our selected TV

Table 3.3 Core themes of fictional women scientists and related interpretation questions that guided analysis with descriptions used to code segments

Theme	Interpretation question	Segment description
Occupation	How is humor used when portraying the expertise and competence of women scientists?	Segments that showed women scientists conducting research in the laboratory, office, or field site; segments where women scientists discuss their research or STEM-related interests; segments where women scientists teach others about STEM; segments where other characters or the narrator comment on the expertise of the women scientist
	How is humor used when portraying the working relationship with male colleagues?	Segments where the women scientist works directly with men; segments where women scientists discuss their interaction with male colleagues
	How is humor used when portraying the work-life balance of women scientists?	Segments where women scientists experience conflict with the work and personal life; segments where women scientists successfully balance their work and personal life; segments where other characters comment on the work-life balance of the women scientist
Stereotype	How is humor used in the portrayal of women scientist stereotypes?	Segments where women scientist characters reflect characteristics and traits of Flicker's (2008) women scientist stereotypes

Theme	Interpretation question	Segment description
	How is humor used in the portrayal of traditional gender stereotypes of women?	Segments where women scientists discuss or reflect traditional beauty standards; segments where other characters comment on traditional beauty standards in relation to the women scientist; Segments where the women scientist or other characters mention traditional gender stereotypes; segments where the women scientist or other characters discuss motherhood in relation to the women scientist; segments where the women scientist or other characters mention traditional gender roles for women

comedies identified important, but commonly overlooked and underexplored cultural themes, thus providing new insights into the contribution of science (communication) cultural history, and food for thought for sharper intellectual agendas.

REFERENCES

Buijzen, M., & Valkenburg, P. M. (2004). Developing a typology of humor in audiovisual media. *Media Psychology*, 6(2), 147–167. https://doi.org/10.1207/s1532785xmep0602_2

Cho, S., Crenshaw, K. W., & McCall, L. (2013). Toward a field of intersectionality studies: Theory, applications, and praxis. *Signs*, 38(4), 785–810. https://doi.org/10.1086/669608

Cooper, B. (2015). Intersectionality. In L. Disch & M. Hawkesworth (Eds.), *The Oxford Handbook of Feminist Theory*, (Vol. 1, Issue August 2019). Oxford University Press. https://doi.org/10.1093/oxfordhb/9780199328581.013.20

Crenshaw, K. (1989). Demarginalizing the intersection of race and sex: A Black feminist critique of antidiscrimination doctrine, feminist theory and antiracist politics. *University of Chicago Legal Forum*, 1989(140), 139–168.

Creswell, J. W. (2014). *Research design: Qualitative, quantitative, and mixed methods approaches*. Sage.

Deater, T. (2021). Navigating women scientist & unnatural selection through: The Nest (1987) and Splice (2006). *International Journal of Fear Studies*, 3(1), 35–44. http://hdl.handle.net/1880/113243

Fitzgerald, T. (2019). *How do "The Big Bang Theory" series finale ratings rank all time?* https://www.forbes.com/sites/tonifitzgerald/2019/05/17/how-does-the-big-bang-theory-series-finale-ratings-rank-all-time/?sh=175a533e386d

Flicker, E. (2008). Women scientists in mainstream film: Social role models—Contribution to the public understanding of science from the perspective of film sociology. In P. Weingart & B. Hüppauf (Eds.), *Science Images and Popular Images of the Sciences*, (pp. 241–256). Routledge.

Grzanka, P. R. (2020). From buzzword to critical psychology: An invitation to take intersectionality seriously. *Women & Therapy*, 43(3–4), 244–261. https://doi.org/10.1080/02703149.2020.1729473

Hailu, S. (2023). *Netflix Top 10: "'Never Have I Ever' final season jumps to first place, 'Black Mirror' season 6 debuts at No. 2"—Variety*. https://variety.com/2023/tv/news/netflix-top-10-never-have-i-ever-black-mirror-1235649714/

Hill Collins, P., & Bilge, S. (2016). *Intersectionality*. Polity Press.

Jensen, P. (1991). Introduction: a qualitative turn. In N. W. Jankowski, & K. B Jensen (Eds.), *A Handbook of Qualitative Methodologies for Mass Communication Research*, (p. 4). https://doi.org/10.4324/9780203409800

Jürgens, A.-S., Darragh, L., Peace, P., Agha, R., Viana, J. N., & Richards, I. (2024). Studying science in pop culture through textual analysis. An introduction to examining science in visual texts—Street art, comics and (animated) film. *Journal of Science Communication*, *23*(03), Y01. https://doi.org/10.22323/2.23030401

Kellner, D. (2020). *Media culture: Cultural studies, identity, and politics in the contemporary moment*. Taylor & Francis.

Kool, D., Azevedo, N. H., & Avraamidou, L. (2022). The lonely heroine: Portrayal of women scientists in films. *Educational Media International*, *59*(2), 150–171. https://doi.org/10.1080/09523987.2022.2101205

Larson, K. B. (1991). Textual analysis of fictional media content. In N. W. Jankowski, K. B. Jensen (Eds.), *A Handbook of Qualitative Methodologies for Mass Communication Research*. Routledge.

McKee, A. (2003). *Textual Analysis: A Beginners Guide*. https://doi.org/10.4135/9780857020017

Never Have I Ever, IMBd, https://www.imdb.com/title/tt10062292/

Otterson, J. (2021, January 6). *"Zoey's Extraordinary playlist" Season 2 premiere hits high in viewers*. Variety. https://variety.com/2021/tv/news/zoeys-extraordinary-playlist-season-2-premiere-ratings-1234879628/

Sagatov, A. I. (2019). *Female scientists in film: Embracing duality with the heroine's journey*. 52. https://scholarworks.montana.edu/xmlui/bitstream/handle/1/15593/SagatovFemaleScientists2019.pdf?sequence=4&isAllowed=y

Steinke, J. (2005). Cultural representations of gender and science: Portrayals of female scientists and engineers in popular films. *Science Communication*, *27*(1), 27–63. https://doi.org/10.1177/1075547005278610

Steinke, J. (2012). Portrayals of female scientists in the mass media. In A. N. Valdivia (Ed.), *The International Encyclopedia of Media Studies*. Wiley. https://doi.org/10.1002/9781444361506.wbiems070

Steinke, J. (2017). Adolescent girls' STEM identity formation and media images of STEM professionals: Considering the influence of contextual cues. *Frontiers in Psychology*, *8*(MAY), 1–15. https://doi.org/10.3389/fpsyg.2017.00716

Steinke, J., & Paniagua Tavarez, P. M. (2017). Cultural representations of gender and STEM: Portrayals of female STEM characters in popular films 2002–2014. *International Journal of Gender, Science and Technology*, *9*(3), 244–277. https://genderandset.open.ac.uk/index.php/genderandset/article/view/514

Su, L.Y.-F., McKasy, M., Cacciatore, M. A., Yeo, S. K., DeGrauw, A. R., & Zhang, J. S. (2022). Generating science buzz: An examination of multidimensional engagement with humorous scientific messages on twitter and instagram. *Science Communication, 44*(1), 30–59. https://doi.org/10.1177/10755470211063902

The Big Bang Theory, IMBd, https://www.imdb.com/title/tt0898266/

Thompson, B., Jürgens, A.-S., None, B., & Lamberts, R. (2023). Street art as a vehicle for environmental science communication. *Journal of Science Communication, 22*(04), A01. https://doi.org/10.22323/2.22040201

Zoey's Extraordinary Playlist, IMBd, https://www.imdb.com/title/tt1031 4462/

"Congrats. Now I Have Two Female Bosses. It's Like I'm Working at Goop": Findings

Abstract This chapter of *Women Scientists in American Television Comedy: Beakers, Big Bangs and Broken Hearts* examines how humor in TV comedies like *Never Have I Ever*, *The Big Bang Theory* and *Zoey's Extraordinary Playlist* communicates and challenges social conventions about science and gender. The analysis reveals that irony (18%) and satire (17%) are the most common humor types used to portray women scientists, often emphasizing their expertise and competence in contrast to their male counterparts. For example, *The Big Bang Theory* uses deadpan and farcical humor to highlight the scientific prowess of characters like Amy Farrah Fowler. Humor also addresses the dynamics between male colleagues and women scientists, often depicting women as superior in competence, though this is not acknowledged by their male peers, using irony, satire and schadenfreude. Additionally, the chapter explores how humor reinforces or challenges stereotypes of women scientists, such as the "old maid" and "gruff women's libber", which suggest that intelligence and femininity are mutually exclusive. Traditional gender stereotypes are also addressed through ironic humor, subverting notions of domesticity and motherhood. The analysis demonstrates that humor in these TV comedies can simultaneously critique and perpetuate gender stereotypes in STEM fields, highlighting the complexities and nuances of these portrayals.

© The Author(s), under exclusive license to Springer Nature
Switzerland AG 2025
K. Judd et al., *Women Scientists in American Television Comedy*,
Palgrave Studies in Science and Popular Culture,
https://doi.org/10.1007/978-3-031-81525-6_4

Keywords Humor and social conventions · Science competence and gender · Science expertise and gender · Humor challenging stereotypes · Femininity and science

This book explored the use of humor to communicate and counter social conventions about science and gender. Our examples revolve around science and, given that they are TV comedies, of course are humorous. But what kind of humor exactly is used and what does it communicate to audiences about women in STEM professions? Is working in a STEM team lead by women really "like I'm working at Goop" (*Zoey's Extraordinary Playlist S01E1*), an enterprise well-known for its anti-science quackery (Claassen, 2020), as a male programmer complains in an episode of our study? Five women scientist characters were identified from the three TV comedies sampled and analyzed: *The Big Bang Theory*, *Never Have I Ever* and *Zoey's Extraordinary Playlist* (see Table 4.1).

The characters that form the basis of this analysis are multifaceted and have varying levels of depth that are generally further developed throughout their arcs on their respective shows. The exception to this is Joan in *Zoey's Extraordinary Playlist*, who is a guest character that did not return for Season 2 of that show, cutting short her storyline compared to the others in this study. All five characters are presented as middle-class, feminine, heterosexual, cisgender women. Amy, Zoey and Joan are white American, while Bernadette is a first-generation American whose parents migrated from Poland. Kamala is an Indian woman studying in the United States for her PhD in biology, living with family members that had previously migrated to America. Bernadette is similarly a PhD student when she debuted on *The Big Bang Theory*, but graduates within the timeline of the show and goes on to get a high-income corporate job, which she later balances with her role as a mother after having children during later

Table 4.1 Overview of women scientist characters

TV show	Women scientist characters
Never Have I Ever	Kamala Nadiwadal
The Big Bang Theory	Amy Farrah Fowler; Bernadette Rostenkowski
Zoey's Extraordinary Playlist	Zoey Clarke; Joan Bennett

seasons. Joan goes through a divorce during her season in *Zoey's Extraordinary Playlist*, while Amy on *The Big Bang Theory* dates multiple men in succession before becoming the partner of the show's main character, Sheldon. Amy, a neurobiology researcher with a PhD, has many traits that have led viewers to speculate that she has Autism Spectrum Disorder, although this is never confirmed on the show (Bialik, 2018). Zoey, as a successful computer programmer, is assumed to have some level of tertiary education, but this is not confirmed on her show, nor is the professional background that lead Joan to the role of Executive Director at SPRQ Point, the fictional organization where they both are employed. Zoey is portrayed as a somewhat anxious person, but most importantly to the plot of the show, she experiences a freak accident which gives her the (magical, superhuman) ability to perceive others' inner thoughts through jukebox-musical-style songs.

When combining all identified humor segments across all TV series, the most common humor types were irony (18%), closely followed by satire (17%), stereotype (11%) and ridicule (10%) (Fig. 4.1). Although there was an array of humor types used across the core themes of fictional women scientists (occupation and stereotypes), the two most dominant humor types were irony and satire in all TV series (Table 4.2). In *The Big Bang Theory*, stereotype humor was equally as dominant as irony and satire but in both *Never Have I Ever* and *Zoey's Extraordinary Playlist* the humor type of ridicule was the third most dominant humor type used in scenes related to the lived experience of the women scientists (Table 4.2).

The research question guiding this book was: **What types of humor characterize portrayals of women scientists in mainstream American comedy television and how is this humor used to shape cultural ideas of (the reality of) women in STEM?** Within this, we divided this overarching question into five sub-questions, each of which we explore below in turn.

How Is Humor Used When Portraying the Expertise and Competence of Women Scientists?

A recurring pattern in representing women scientists' expertise and competence was the use of humor during explicit portrayals of their STEM-related work. In *The Big Bang Theory*, scenes that establish the

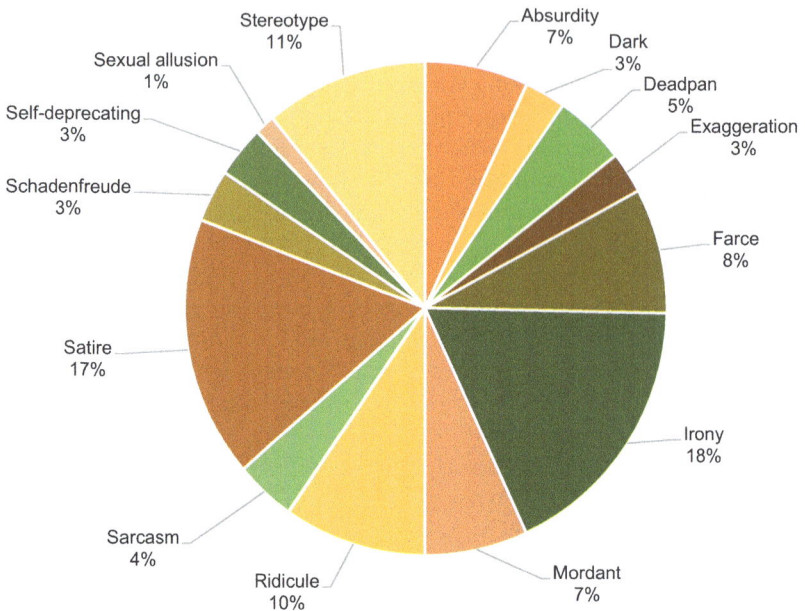

Fig. 4.1 Composition of humor types used in scenes related to core themes of the women scientist character across all three TV series

women scientists' expertise and competence typically depict the characters conducting scientific experiments and working in a laboratory environment. Such experiments commonly involve elements of farcical and ironic humor, generally associated with the woman scientist character and their scientific research. For example, in *The Big Bang Theory*, Amy, a neurobiologist, conducts research where she "recently trained a capuchin monkey to smoke cigarettes" (*The Herb Garden Germination*, S04E20). In later episodes, Amy is then shown in the laboratory conducting an experiment examining the responses of a monkey shown images of a "Frenchman on a bicycle carrying baguettes", "a sousaphone" and a "crocodile with a mouthful of monkeys" (*The Workplace Proximity*, S07E5). Already humorous with farcical humor resulting from the exaggerated nature of the scientific research, the scene introduces another layer of humor with Sheldon, Amy's partner and fellow scientist, exhibiting the same responses as the monkey, adding an element of satirical humor. Rarely is the specific

Table 4.2 Composition of humor types in each TV series sample by percentage

	Percentage of humor types in each TV series (%)		
	Never Have I Ever	The Big Bang Theory	Zoey's Extraordinary Playlist
Absurdity	3.2	5.2	10.5
Dark	0.0	5.2	1.8
Deadpan	0.0	6.9	5.3
Exaggeration	3.2	5.2	0.0
Farce	9.7	10.3	5.3
Irony	25.8	15.5	15.8
Mordant	3.2	13.8	1.8
Ridicule	16.1	3.4	12.3
Sarcasm	3.2	0.0	8.8
Satire	19.4	15.5	17.5
Schadenfreude	0.0	1.7	7.0
Self-deprecating	3.2	0.0	7.0
Sexual allusion	0.0	1.7	1.8
Stereotype	12.9	15.5	5.3
Absurdity	3.2	5.2	10.5

scientific research explained beyond the superficial; rather, the scientific elements are used as a platform for humor, with the topics being inherently humorous or humorous due to the character's level of engagement or interest. In other episodes, humor is derived from the woman scientist's own engagement and discussion of topics that assert her scientific expertise. Amy frequently mentions her own research, however, due to her expressionless and serious tone, the delivery of the dialogue renders the scene humorous through the use of deadpan humor. For example, Amy tells her fellow scientist friends that the Neurology Department loaned her a culture of prions for her research on "bovine spongiform encephalopathy" (*The Isolation Permutation*, S05E8). Although bovine spongiform encephalopathy (the scientific name of mad cow disease) is not inherently humorous, Amy's deadpan expression simultaneously acts as a humorous device, while also demonstrating her expertise as a neurobiologist.

In establishing their expertise and competence, the women scientist characters are humorously contrasted to other characters, especially those who also possess STEM expertise. In both *The Big Bang Theory* and *Never Have I Ever*, the women scientists inform a friend or colleague of their academic achievements or scientific interests only to be overtly dismissed by a less important or trivial comment by another character. Although the woman scientist is dismissed and often humiliated in these situations, the humor is typically a result of irony and satire, as opposed to being based on schadenfreude, thereby criticizing the other character and not the woman scientist. For example, in *The Big Bang Theory*, Amy tells her partner and fellow scientist, Sheldon, that her most recent paper "on how cooperative long-term potentiation can map memory sequences in dendritic branches" made the cover of a scientific journal (*The Shiny Trinket Manoeuvre*, S05E12). The dialogue establishes both her competence and expertise in her field, however, it is contrasted by Sheldon disregarding Amy's news, only to focus on his more trivial achievement of "100 Twitter followers" (*The Shiny Trinket Maneuver*, S05E12). The scene is humorous through its use of irony, as the audience recognizes that Amy's achievement is far superior, despite Sheldon believing the opposite. In *Never Have I Ever*, ironic humor is also used to portray Kamala's competence compared to her supervisor's immaturity. Although demonstrating her expertise in the laboratory setting, her supervisor does not recognize her scientific findings until she feigns enthusiasm in an unrelated K-Pop band 'BLACKPINK', where he then acknowledges her hard work and rewards her with the day off (*...had an Indian* frenemy, S02E4). In *Zoey's Extraordinary Playlist*, Zoey's competence as a software developer and leader is portrayed through humorous comparisons to her less competent male colleagues. Zoey is frequently praised for her managerial and leadership skills, while her male colleagues are portrayed implementing childish games in the workplace (*Zoey's Extraordinary Return*, S02E1). The farcical and satirical humor associated with the immaturity of Zoey's male colleagues, emphasizes her superior leadership expertise.

How Is Humor Used When Portraying the Working Relationship Between Women Scientists and Male Colleagues?

In all three TV series, the women scientists are frequently positioned as superior to their male counterparts from the audience's perspective, however, this belief is not shared by the male characters, resulting in humorous failures and humiliation through irony, satire and schadenfreude. For example, in *The Big Bang Theory*, Amy has Sheldon, a theoretical physicist, work in her neurobiology lab (*The Vacation Solution*, S05E16). Given the laboratory is not his area of expertise, she gives him lower-level tasks such as cleaning beakers, which he at first refuses to do, comparing it to "asking The Incredible Hulk to open a pickle jar" (*The Vacation Solution*, S05E16). Sheldon becomes defensive after Amy criticizes the job; however, she challenges him to drink from the beaker that previously contained "cerebrospinal fluid from an elephant that died of syphilis" (*The Vacation Solution*, S05E16). Reluctantly he goes to repeat the task, humorously muttering to himself "biologists are mean" as he walks away humiliated (*The Vacation Solution*, S05E16). A similar display of defensiveness with the use of schadenfreude is seen in *Zoey's Extraordinary Playlist* when a male programmer yells out to his colleagues "two more hours, and I would've gotten it, just saying" after Zoey solved a programming error (*Zoey's Extraordinary Power*, S01E1). Later in the episode, the same male colleague sarcastically congratulates Zoey on her promotion to Manager of Engineering saying, "congrats. Now I have two female bosses. It's like I'm working at Goop" (*Zoey's Extraordinary Power*, S01E1). In *Never Have I Ever*, Kamala jokes about the inferiority of her male supervisor when plotting her revenge after he does not credit her discovery (*...begged for forgiveness*, S02E7). Kamala is depicted texting another colleague, "tell me all of Evan's weaknesses. I assume there are many", establishing Evan's inferiority through satire (*...begged for forgiveness*, S02E7).

The use of humor is also pronounced in scenes related to sexism in workplace environments dominated by men. Sexism pervades through both ironic jokes made by male colleagues and statements by women scientists who describe other characters as sexist. Ironic sexism in the form of superficially benign jokes is particularly prevalent in *Zoey's Extraordinary Playlist*, with a workplace of all young male programmers under the authority of two women. Male programmers are seen making ironic jokes in the workplace in reference to their female colleagues such as: "A woman's place is in the house and the Senate... What up!" and "I thought you'd be buying matching tote bags off Etsy in there". In one episode Zoey is seen trying to boost team productivity by giving everyone a journal, which she is met by sarcasm from her male colleague: "Oh cool. I've always wanted a diary. Are you there, God? It's me, Tobin" (*Zoey's Extraordinary Best Friend*, S01E2), referencing Judy Blume's

American novel popular with teenage girls. Through the humor types of sarcasm and stereotype, Zoey is mocked by her male colleagues who, in reference to the journals, state "if it's from 'Sisterhood of the Traveling Pants', please do not spoil the ending" (*Zoey's Extraordinary Best Friend*, S012). The prevalence of sexism by her male colleagues is also overtly stated when Zoey requests to know her colleagues' feedback on an anonymous peer review, insisting "I'm sure the team had thoughts" (*Zoey's Extraordinary Failure*, S01E5). However, her boss, who is also a female programmer, refuses to disclose her feedback but confirms in a sarcastic manner that it was indeed shrouded in sexism: "Oh 'the team had thoughts' but you know, 'misogyny, misogyny.' I think you're crushing it. That's all that matters" (*Zoey's Extraordinary Failure*, S01E5). In *Never Have I Ever*, Kamala's experience with sexism in the workplace is also communicated with humor, starting from the first day of her new Ph.D. rotation where she is stereotyped for her appearance. Her supervisor uses self-deprecating humor in his stereotyping of her, asking "You probably have, like, a really handsome boyfriend, huh? Sorry you have to work with a bunch of gross nerds like us", to which Kamala politely and genuinely responds "That's not true. You're not gross"—followed by ironic humor where she is interrupted by a male colleague burping (...*been a playa*, S02E1).

How Is Humor Used When Portraying the Work-Life Balance of Women Scientists?

The balancing of professional and personal life as a woman scientist was addressed through humor in all three television series. Schadenfreude and ironic humor were the most common humor types prevalent in sequences addressing this idea, as sequences often focus on the misfortune of the woman scientist and her failures in maintaining a work-life balance. An example of how schadenfreude humor is used to allude to this notion can be seen in *Zoey's Extraordinary Playlist*. After being confronted by the prospect of a romantic relationship with her best friend, Max, Zoey instead throws herself into her work and stays up all night to work on a project that had previously been delegated to her whole team (*Zoey's Extraordinary Best Friend*, S01E2). A series of unfortunate, but humorous, events through schadenfreude humor, ensues, as she is woken up at her desk the next day with disheveled hair and drool around her mouth, only to get up and have cups of coffee spilled all over her (*Zoey's*

Extraordinary Best Friend, S01E2). In later episodes, Zoey struggles to balance her personal and professional life while also being pursued romantically by two of her co-workers (*Zoey's Extraordinary Glitch*, S01E8). Zoey's turmoil due to her work-life imbalance is represented through the humor types of absurdity and schadenfreude, where she uncontrollably sings in an important presentation to the CEO of her company (*Zoey's Extraordinary Glitch*, S01E8).

In *The Big Bang Theory*, Amy is faced with the decision to advance her career by taking a fellowship position at Princeton University or risk her relationship with Sheldon (*The Gyroscopic Collapse*, S10E23). Amy is depicted seeking advice from her friend, Penny, who tells her "come on, he's a grown man, he can take care of himself" to which Amy quickly replies "You really believe that?" (*The Gyroscopic Collapse*, S10E23). The mordant and ridiculing humor alludes to Sheldon's child-like dependence on Amy, but also serves as comic relief to the decision Amy is faced with, choosing her career at the cost of her relationship (*The Gyroscopic Collapse*, S10E23). In *Never Have I Ever*, the humorous portrayal of the struggle to maintain relationships and work is frequently represented. After commencing her new Ph.D. rotation, Kamala is seen struggling to maintain her relationship with her boyfriend, being required to work extra hours. For example, on a rare occasion she has time off work for a date night with her boyfriend, however, mid-date, her supervisor calls her to say "I was doing this spot-on impression of Neo in The Matrix, dodging bullets, and I knocked over a bunch of your samples, so we need you to come back and redo them" (*...had an Indian frenemy*, S02E4). The satirical and ironic humor of the scene is directed at the foolishness of her supervisor, however, ultimately the situation depicts her difficulty in maintaining a relationship while pursuing her Ph.D.

How Is Humor Used in the Portrayal of Women Scientist Stereotypes?

Humor aids in depicting Amy as two of Flicker's (2008) women scientist stereotypes: the "old maid" and the "gruff women's libber". Amy physically embodies these stereotypes by wearing knee-length skirts, knitted vests and button-down shirts, unlike the other women in the series who wear bright colors and casual clothes more befitting their age. As a result, she is often ridiculed for her choice of attire. For example, Amy is seen moving into her friend Penny's apartment due to a leaking pipe in her apartment (*The Cohabitation Experiment*, S10E4). Penny asks her "Did you lose anything valuable?" to which Amy replies "Well, the pipe was over my closet so all of my clothes are gone" (*The Contractual Obligation Implementation*, S06E18). Penny then replies "Oh, so nothing..." which is followed by a laugh track, highlighting through mordant humor that the opinion that Amy has a poor fashion sense is shared by the audience. Another characteristic of the "old maid" stereotype according to Flicker (2003, p. 311) is being "only interested in her work, as though she were married to it", which is humorously embodied with Amy's deadpan and serious tone when engaging with science. Amy, and the humor associated with her character, also reflects the stereotype of the "gruff women's libber" which consists of a loss of femininity, a rough harsh voice and practical clothing (Flicker 2003, p. 311).

The ironic sexist humor used in *Never Have I Ever* often incorporates common ideas involved in the women scientist stereotypes of the "old maid" and "gruff women's libber". Both of these women scientist stereotypes perpetuate the notion that for women scientists, intelligence and femininity are mutually exclusive (Flicker, 2003, 2008). For example, Kamala is depicted expressing her enthusiasm and expertise as a scientist, which is not understood by her younger cousin, Devi, who tells her "It is so annoying how no one knows how nerdy you are because you're so hot", to which Kamala replies a very genuine, "Thank you Devi" (*...been a playa*, S02E1). Kamala, both glamorously attractive (without being portrayed as superficial) and an active scientist, struggles to comfortably reconcile these apparently competing aspects of herself, instead separating herself into somewhat distinct home and work personalities, while also navigating cultural values and expectations as an Indian-American woman. Her intersectional experiences of sexism combined with racism are depicted as a source of challenges for Kamala while presenting the audience with moments of humor and sympathy.

A feature of many women scientist stereotypes is the idea that women scientists are unable to find love and relationships (Flicker 2003, 2008). Instances of humor conveying this idea were present in both *The Big Bang Theory* and *Zoey's Extraordinary Playlist*. For example, in *The Big Bang Theory*, this idea is portrayed through ironic sexist humor when Sheldon suggests that he and Amy go on a children's television program "Professor Proton" "to show that even female scientists can land a man" (*The Novelisation Correlation*, S11E15). Meanwhile in *Zoey's Extraordinary Playlist* deadpan humor is used to describe the failures in Zoey and Joan's, two software engineers, relationships. Zoey's past and failed relationships are called "unnecessarily complicated, exhausting for everybody, the opposite of good" (*Zoey's Extraordinary Power*, S01E1). In a later episode, Joan and Zoey discuss Joan's failing marriage, after which she tells Zoey, "It really helped me see some of the inefficiencies in my relationship and I have a solid game plan now moving forward to ensure proper marital growth" (*Zoey's Extraordinary Boss*, S01E3). The humorous robotic deadpan delivery of such a personal topic alludes to a likely failure of Joan's marriage. While most of the women scientists in our study often lack qualities of traditional femininity and romantic relationships at the cost of scientific expertise, Kamala embodies the "lonely heroine" stereotype, who is highly competent, likable, attractive and successful in romantic pursuits (Flicker, 2003, 2008). However, as per the stereotype, she lacks professional recognition, which is humorously portrayed throughout the program, using humor types of irony and absurdity.

How Is Humor Used in the Portrayal of Traditional Gender Stereotypes of Women?

In all three TV series, ironic humor is incorporated into dialogue to allude to traditional beauty standards and feminine stereotypes. In *The Big Bang Theory*, the two women scientist characters are seen visiting Disneyland (*The Contractual Obligation Implementation*, S06E18). However, while dressed as Disney Princesses they are asked to address a class of middle school girls over the phone about pursuing a career in science (*The Contractual Obligation Implementation*, S06E18). Amy then tells the students, "The world of science needs more women but from a young age we girls are encouraged to care more about the way we look than about the power of her mind" (*The Contractual Obligation Implementation*, S06E18). There is significant ironic humor in the scene as Amy is saying this while dressed as Disney Princesses, applying lipstick and looking at their reflections in the mirror (*The Contractual Obligation Implementation*, S06E18). In *Zoey's Extraordinary Playlist*, ironic humor is also used to reference traditional women's stereotypes, however, in the form of ironic sexism. In the first episode of the series, Zoey is interviewed for a position as Manager of Engineering (*Zoey's Extraordinary Power*, S01E1). After the interview, she tells her male colleagues that the interview did not go well, to which one replies "Really? I thought you'd be doing each other's nails and buying matching tote bags off Etsy in there" (*Zoey's Extraordinary Power*, S01E1). The sarcastic but sexist joke is followed by another male colleague saying "Dude, come on. Not cool" (*Zoey's Extraordinary Power*, S01E1). Although the comment is superficially rebuked, the joke is still found humorous as it alludes to underlying stereotypes of women.

Using the typology of humor developed by Buijzen and Valkenburg (2004), our analysis uncovered that various humor types, most notably irony, were used to subvert traditional stereotypes involving the 'instinctive' domestic and maternal qualities of women. This pattern was only identified in episodes of *The Big Bang Theory*, however, the women scientist characters of the other two programs were slightly younger, therefore topics of motherhood were less salient. The character of Bernadette humorously expresses on several occasions her concerns about becoming a mother, often through dark humor. While heavily pregnant, she tells her friend, Raj, that "Not every girl dreams about being a mom. Sometimes you think you're never gonna have kids and one day you wake up and you're pregnant and it doesn't matter that your career is going great right now and that you and your husband never got to go anywhere" (*The Dependence Transcendence*, S10E3). In a later scene, Raj assures Bernadette that she's "gonna be an amazing mom. Even if you don't believe it, I know you have maternal instincts", to which Bernadette responds, "Once I was supposed to babysit my brothers. Our neighbors found them naked in our backyard eating crickets" (*The Dependence Transcendence*, S10E3). Amy also shares a similar hesitance to be a mother when her partner, Sheldon, tries to coerce Amy into having children (*The Brain Bowl Incubation*, S10E8). After Sheldon's failed attempts to seduce Amy, he tells her "I don't understand. I thought you'd be thrilled to procreate with me" to which Amy shouts "Not right now" and storms out of the room, which is followed by a laugh track (*The Brain Bowl Incubation*, S10E8). Sheldon's failed attempts and ultimate rejection by Amy establish a sense of mordant humor, while also challenging traditional gender-based stereotypes of motherhood as a desire and priority for women.

References

Bialik, M. (2018, November 20). *Mayim discusses the use of labels on 'The Big Bang Theory'*. Grok Nation. https://groknation.com/culture/the-big-bang-theory-labels-mayim-bialik/

Buijzen, M., & Valkenburg, P. M. (2004). Developing a typology of humor in audiovisual media. *Media Psychology, 6*(2), 147–167. https://doi.org/10.1207/s1532785xmep0602_2

Claassen, G. (2020). The quackery virus: A preliminary analysis of pseudo-scientific health messages on Twitter. In P. Weingart, M. Joubert, & B. Falade (Eds.), *Science Communication in Africa: Reflections on Current Issues*. African Minds.

Flicker, E. (2003). Between brains and breasts—Women scientists in fiction film: On the marginalization and sexualization of scientific competence. *Public Understanding of Science, 12*(3), 307–318. https://doi.org/10.1177/0963662503123009

Flicker, E. (2008). Women scientists in mainstream film: Social role models—Contribution to the public understanding of science from the perspective of film sociology. In P. Weingart & B. Hüppauf (Eds.), *Science Images and Popular Images of the Sciences*, (pp. 241–256). Routledge.

CHAPTER 5

"It Is So Annoying How No One Knows How Nerdy You Are Because You're So Hot": Discussion

Abstract This chapter of *Women Scientists in American Television Comedy: Beakers, Big Bangs and Broken Hearts* discusses the analysis of 47 episodes from *Never Have I Ever*, *The Big Bang Theory* and *Zoey's Extraordinary Playlist* focusing on how humor types such as irony and satire are used to portray women scientists. These humor types, aligning with the Superiority Theory, often involve outwitting others and ridiculing male characters, highlighting the women scientists' intellectual and social superiority and reflecting feminist humor's subversive nature. The study found that satire and irony, more appreciated by a general and adolescent audience, were prevalent, with farcical humor also commonly used to depict scientific work humorously. Humor is also used to address gender biases in workplace dynamics, with male colleagues often dismissing women scientists, thereby mirroring real-world gender biases in STEM fields. The portrayal of work-life balance struggles for women scientists frequently employs schadenfreude and ironic humor, emphasizing the stereotype that women must choose between a career in STEM and their personal life. Additionally, humor derived from traditional gender stereotypes challenges their femininity and reinforces the incongruity of motherhood and STEM careers. The concept of the comic frame is used to examine how these shows employ humor as a tool to distance the audience, allowing viewers to engage critically with gendered stereotypes of women in science. Despite some positive portrayals, the

© The Author(s), under exclusive license to Springer Nature Switzerland AG 2025
K. Judd et al., *Women Scientists in American Television Comedy*, Palgrave Studies in Science and Popular Culture, https://doi.org/10.1007/978-3-031-81525-6_5

humor often perpetuates stereotypes, potentially influencing young girls' perceptions of STEM careers negatively. However, feminist humor in these shows also serves to critique and subvert patriarchal norms. This chapter illustrates both the empowering and limiting potential of comedic representation in shaping societal attitudes toward women scientists.

Keywords Irony · Satire · Science work-life balance · Incongruity · Feminist humor

Women scientists are complex characters that can be both "nerdy" and "hot" (*Never Have I Ever, S02E1*)—and so much more. In this discussion chapter, we relate the findings of Chapter 4 to the broader landscape of women in STEM and humor on television, and examine that while feminist humor is employed to subvert patriarchal norms, portrayals of traditional gender roles can also reinforce them. Finally, this chapter provides a discussion of comic framing through close reading of the women scientist characters of the study.

The Use of Humor Around Women in STEM—A Feminist Pursuit?

Our analysis of 47 episodes of *Never Have I Ever, The Big Bang Theory* and *Zoey's Extraordinary Playlist* showed that the most common humor types used in relation to the women scientist characters in these TV comedies were irony and satire. According to Buijzen and Valkenburg's (2004) humor typology, these humor types belong to the Superiority Theory, as they involve outwitting others and laughing at the misfortunes of others. Buijzen and Valkenburg argue that satire and irony, being more complex humor categories, appeal more to a general and adolescent audience, likely due to these age groups having a greater appreciation for more sophisticated forms of humor (Acuff & Reiher, 1997), while also appealing to the non-compliant attitude of adolescents (Buijzen & Valkenburg, 2004). When comparing humor aimed at different gender groups, in their study, adult women tended to appreciate nonsensical and silly humor, like that of slapstick, than men (Buijzen & Valkenburg, 2004, p. 152). These insights are consistent with previous studies of humor preferences, which suggest men prefer more caustic and disparaging humor (e.g. irony and satire), while women prefer innocent humor categories (e.g. clownish humor and surprise, Brodzinsky et al., 1981; Johnson, 1992). This is interesting, as while our study found that the women scientist characters serve as both the humorous subject and vehicle to humorously ridicule others (frequently male characters or patriarchal structures), according to Buijzen and Valkenburg (2004) this humor may not be directed for a female audience. Indeed, women are the object, not the audience for instances of humor with sexist undertones—even when ironic (Drakett et al., 2018; Woodzicka & Ford, 2010). However, as our findings show, scenes that use the humor types of irony, satire, ridicule and schadenfreude typically criticize male characters and portray the women scientist as intellectually and socially superior, demonstrating its feminist aims. However, as Riquelme et al. (2023) have more recently argued, humor disparaging men is not necessarily automatically feminist. Instead, truly feminist humor subverts sexism against all genders, critiquing patriarchal society in the process. Therefore, humor that *only* is disparaging toward men in comparison to women may be feminist, but is not always inherently so.

In portraying the expertise and competence of the women scientist, farcical and ironic were the most common humor types. These occurred in situations where the scientist was engaged in her work and compared to other, typically male, scientists. As identified in our findings, the science that the women scientists engage in is a short-lived comment and not explained beyond the superficial. This is consistent with past work on *The Big Bang Theory* by Fairweather (2019) found that the women scientists' (Amy and Bernadette's) scientific work was typically portrayed only for dramatic or comedic effect, with many episodes failing the Bechdel test. The irony of scenes targeting and ridiculing the male characters is consistent with the constructs of feminist humor. This subversive and rebellious form of humor criticizes and exposes patriarchal structures and challenges traditional gendered views by targeting men and opposing dominant constructs of femininity (Barreca, 1991; Crawford, 2003; Franzini, 1996). In *Zoey's Extraordinary Playlist*, the farcical and satirical humor associated with the immaturity of the male colleagues in comparison to Zoey emphasizes her superior leadership expertise. In establishing Zoey's expertise, the ridicule of the male colleague also serves as an example of feminist humor, by encouraging the audience to question patriarchal power structures (Riquelme et al., 2023; Shifman & Lemish, 2010). Interestingly, in their comparison of humor types across genders,

Buijzen and Valkenburg (2004) identified that satire was the humor type used the least in commercials aimed at women and girls. Assuming the feminist humor in *Zoey's Extraordinary Playlist* and *Never Have I Ever* is aimed at women, satire emerges as one of the most common humor types, thereby challenging Buijzen and Valkenburg's (2004) findings.

Examples of such satirical humor were found to involve other characters dismissing the expertise of the women scientists, despite the audience recognizing the skill and expertise of the women scientist. In other findings relating to the use of humor in portrayals of relationships between men and women in a workplace, humor was commonly derived from male colleagues not perceiving women scientists to be equal or superior despite their merit. This mirrors the experience of women in the workplace generally who are not respected as superior, suffering from stereotypical gender bias around women's suitability for leadership (Eagly, 2007), being criticized more when providing negative feedback (Abel, 2024), and experience resentment from male colleagues and subordinates (Netchaeva et al., 2015). This also plays out in STEM workplaces, with senior scientists perceiving junior women scientists as less committed to their work than their male colleagues at a similar level—despite no evidence for such a claim—with senior women holding these views in particular (Ellemers et al., 2004). However, Haas et al. (2016) argue that whether women in the laboratory take on masculine or feminine identities, it is structural change that is needed to holistically support their career. In light of our results, we therefore wonder whether feminist humor, and its discourses, could be a tool for starting difficult conversations about the need for disruptive change in a way that both highlights existing problems while easing the delivery on those who feel like they will lose cultural status and privilege?

In a more covert form of dismissal, our findings identified that interactions between men and women featured the humor device of ironic sexism, which was most notable in *Zoey's Extraordinary Playlist*. Ironic sexism allows for the expression of sexist views without claiming ownership and responsibility of such views by adopting both anti-feminist and feminist discourses (Benwell, 2007; Drakett et al., 2018; Gill, 2007; Greenwood & Isbell, 2002; Worth et al., 2016). As a form of disparagement humor, ironic sexist humor can replace a non-prejudiced social norm with a norm of tolerance of sexism, and provide a loophole to which individuals can freely express anti-feminist sentiments without fears of reprisal (Cole, 2015; Ford et al., 2001, 2013, 2017). For decades, research into non-fictional science environments has described what the television episodes portray a "chilly climate" (Hall & Sandler, 1982) of subtle and overt sexism and its subsequent impact on the ability of girls and women to flourish in science, with these experiences continuing to be commonplace today (e.g. Britton, 2017). These phenomena illustrate once again the power of popular entertainment in shaping our conceptions of science-related social realities and the role of mass media in constructing meanings of and around science (cf. Flicker, 2008, p. 242; Jürgens, 2024). If the purpose of ironic sexist humor is ultimately to silence women and keep them 'in their place' in outdated gender roles in society (Cole, 2015), this presumably also suggests that women don't 'really' belong in STEM. This subtle messaging should be challenged even when we're laughing.

The portrayal of the work-life balance of women scientists most frequently used schadenfreude and ironic humor to focus on the misfortunes and failures in 'having it all'. The mutual exclusivity of a career in STEM and the personal life of women scientists is a stereotype that has dominated media in both fictional and non-fictional settings (LaFollette, 1988; Mitchell & McKinnon, 2019; Steinke, 2012). Amy's experiences in *The Big Bang Theory* can be read in light of research showing that women in science careers struggle with balancing their careers with the pressures of their partner's career—especially when that partner is also in science—with or without children (e.g. Bell et al., 2015; Dasgupta & Stout, 2014; Hewlett et al., 2008; Rosser, 2018). Women in science interviewed by Bell et al. (2015) commented on how science careers were set up for a man who had a wife to take care of things at home, allowing the male scientist to focus on creating a laboratory environment that attracts and celebrates other men with similar features. This self-perpetuating system, which is represented fictionally in the TV series (both *The Big Bang Theory* and *Never Have I Ever* show this explicitly in their plotlines), has changed little to match modern dual-career family dynamics (let alone single parents or complex home contexts) and an increasingly diverse workforce, and is often noted as an area of opportunity to improve retention of women in science. Like many of the women scientist stereotypes, these negative stereotypes can be damaging to the perceptions of young girls and have implications for the uptake of STEM careers (Mitchell & McKinnon, 2019, pp. 177, 178; Steele, 1997; Steinke, 2005; Yıldırım et al., 2021). It is disappointing to see schadenfreude and ironic humor used when the women scientists and engineer characters in our sample do try to succeed in the work and personal aspects of their lives concurrently, at times subtly reinforcing through humor that they—and the girls and women interested in STEM watching these shows—shouldn't be so ambitious.

Our findings show that across our sample, humor is used in the portrayal of many of Flicker's (2008) women scientist stereotypes, most frequently the "old maid" and the "gruff women's libber". These two stereotypes are characterized by higher scientific competence at the expense of traditional femininity, whereby the "old maid" dresses in an "old fashioned" style (Flicker, 2003, p. 331, cf. 2008), and the "gruff women's libber" is defined by a loss of femininity and erotic appeal (Flicker, 2008, p. 247). Despite this, representations of women scientists in our sampled TV shows transgressed other women scientist stereotypes, and showed women in positions of power: confident, skilled, driven and knowledgeable, serving as positive role models even when themes of appearance and romance coincide with their portrayal. They could be desirable, even 'hot'—as Kamala is explicitly described in *Never Have I Ever*, for example. In addition, humor related to traditional women stereotypes was frequently found in the context of motherhood. The emphasis of women scientists as mothers have been heavily identified in past media analyses, with the assertion that even successful women scientists are more fulfilled by motherhood than research (LaFollette, 1988; Shachar, 2000). Studies have shown that working women scientists do experience a 'motherhood penalty' which can set back or permanently redirect their careers in ways that men and childless women do not experience (e.g. Eren, 2022; Herman, 2009). On the other hand, women in STEM have been found to reject or self-silence aspects of traditional gender and maternal identities in environments where they perceive their gender to be a potential threat; as a consequence, women experience lower confidence, decreased engagement with their work and opportunities to progress, and hold heightened expectations of bias or discrimination (Ahlqvist et al., 2013; London et al., 2012). The perceived incongruity of motherhood and STEM is humorously reflected in *The Big Bang Theory* to represent the struggles faced by women in this position. This quality of comedy to unite amid adversity is articulated by Andy Medhurst (2007, p. 19), who describes comedy as a "brief embrace in a threatening world, a moment of unity in a lifetime of fissures, a haven against insecurity, a refuge from dissolution, a point of wholesomeness in a maelstrom of fragmentation, a chance to affirm that you exist and that you matter". These comedic portrayals, then, are a positive signal of some diversification and deepening of the image of the woman scientist.

Although many of the women scientist characters are portrayed more realistically—with impressive careers, achievements, extensive personal life, interests, hobbies and skills—humor is frequently derived from allusions to stereotypes of women scientists and women in general. Humor types have been shown to be important in the portrayal of various women scientist stereotypes found in media (Flicker, 2003, 2008) and in non-fictional contexts (e.g. Banchefsky et al., 2016; Ellemers et al., 2004; Francis et al., 2017; Gheorghiu et al., 2017). The perpetuation of such stereotypes can be damaging to audiences—in particular, young girls—as they may internalize such stereotypes, developing negative attitudes about a career in STEM (Mitchell & McKinnon, 2019; Steinke, 2012). And we found similarities in our sample in the way that humorous depictions often reflected that of real-world experiences of gender discrimination. The women in the TV series that we studied were consistently taken less seriously than the men around them, and worked harder for fewer rewards. Yet humor types that are common to feminist humor (e.g. satire and irony), also served as a platform to challenge and subvert traditional stereotypes and ridicule patriarchal power structures. This reflects McIntosh's (2014) analysis of the women scientists in *The Big Bang Theory*, who concluded that due to the primary function of situational comedies to entertain, and occasions where the women scientist stereotype is challenged is only superficial, leading to the continuation of the status quo (McIntosh, 2014, p. 196). Further, although Weitekamp (2015) praises *The Big Bang Theory* for offering more nuanced and depth to its representation of scientists, women characters fall victim to the Matilda Effect (Rossiter, 1993; see Chapter 2) where their achievements are minimized and framed against the men in their lives. Additionally, many of their humorous characteristics derive from a Western understanding of gender norms. Like Soucy-Humphreys et al. (2023)'s study of women scientists in children's television, we found that the women in all three series we studied generally adhered to certain notions of femininity, with humorous moments arising when these rules of gender were transgressed.

This flattening, or "symbolic annihilation" (Tuchman, 2000, p. 150) of the women scientists into foils, love interests and other roles that support male characters' plotlines reduces not only the cultural understanding of women scientists, but of the culture of science in general. Kirby (2011, p. 223) aptly states that

Scientists focus on questions of "how?" which is useful for filmmakers in setting constraints. But, scientists also consistently ask the more artistically inclined questions of "why?" and "what if?" Scientists, like artists, are trying to create narrative explanations about the world. Speculation, synthesis, integration, and problem solving are all creative skills that filmmakers rely upon when they bring scientific experts into productions. These abilities complement scientists' expertise of logic, allowing them to add plausibility to a film's narrative, speculative scenarios, and fantastical situations.

Women scientists—and indeed all STEM professionals—are more complex and nuanced than these TV portrayals suggest. Modern portrayals of science as something that people do, rather than being their _entire_ identity, provides an opportunity for filmmakers and creators to illustrate more intersectional experiences. Kamala in _Never Have I Ever_ is a particularly good example of this, as she navigates various plot points related to not only her gender and her STEM career, but how these interface with her familial and romantic relationships, her personal ambitions and her cultural values and practices.

DEFINING THE COMIC WOMAN SCIENTIST WITHIN A COMIC FRAME

How, then, can the 'comic woman scientist' be defined? The following key characteristics emerged from our analysis and discussion of women scientists in selected episodes of the TV comedies _The Big Bang Theory_, _Never Have I Ever_ and _Zoey's Extraordinary Playlist_:

a. Expressions of humor—irony and satire in particular—shape what science is in comedy shows featuring women scientists. The interface between science and humor is an arena for the confrontation and identification of different cultural and STEM-related references about the woman-(in)-science relationship. However, it is not science or the way science is done that is comic, but the woman scientist's engagement with or interest in it—and how she is humorously stereotyped by her male environment.

b. The experience of women scientists is at the heart of their humorous portrayals. Humor shapes the way women scientists try (and fail) to balance their professional and personal lives, especially in terms of their romantic relationships.

c. While the woman scientist is positioned as superior to her male counterparts (from the audience's perspective), the humor comes from the male characters ignoring or not understanding her, resulting in humorous failure and humiliation through irony, satire and schadenfreude. The lack of professional recognition is rocket fuel for comedy. The challenges of working with male colleagues lead to humor, as does the ridicule of misogynistic attitudes in the workplace.

These characteristics alone, we hasten to add, do not appear in a contextual vacuum. Beyond the humor used at the level of character creation, development and interaction, our three series employ different kinds of playful framing—comic frames—indicating that we, the audience, are allowed to laugh at, and in some cases with, the comic woman scientists. As we know from comedy studies, comic frames enable us to laugh, to enjoy the downfall of others, the overthrow of dignity and ambition, and to see protagonists ridiculed and hurt (psychologically or even physically) without 'real' consequences—because, well, "[m]any human beings are intrinsically nasty" (Peacock, 2020, p. 75). For example, slapstick performances in the circus, where clowns hit each other with humongous hammers and piles of bricks, or saw each other in half with gigantic musical instruments, are manifested within the comic frame of the circus, a space we recognize as one of amusement, if not hyperbolic performance (Jürgens, 2024), signaling a lack of consequence "integral to encouraging a laughter response to the depiction of pain" (Peacock, 2014, p. 142). Louise Peacock further explains:

> The audience are therefore not encouraged to make any empathetic or psychologically nuanced connection with any of the performers. In the case of the clowns this distancing effect is further enhanced by their make-up, red noses, extravagant hair and outlandish costumes. (Peacock, 2014, p. 87)

The lack of reality embodied by clowns contributes to the comic frame and "frees us to respond a laughter untrammeled by any moral considerations" (Peacock, 2020, p. 75). As Daniel Hessler points out in discussing Peacock's definition, recognizing this type of comic frame (as with other types) requires a certain degree of cultural knowledge in order to contextualize "aesthetic cues" and conventions (Hessler, 2020, 90). While the TV comedies *The Big Bang Theory*, *Never Have I Ever* and *Zoey's Extraordinary Playlist* are obviously not circus shows, their scientist protagonists unfold within comic frames that prompt critical reflection on the multifaceted effects of distancing and immersion as they affect not only our perception of humor, but also how we perceive science- and scientist-related content, references and dynamics; with comic frames characterized by canned laughter, absurdist dance routines and cultural critique.

THE COMIC FRAME OF CANNED LAUGHTER AND THE WOMAN SCIENTIST

The comic frame and, by extension, audience expectation, in *The Big Bang Theory* is firmly established by a laugh track, also known as 'canned laughter', which signposts the show as utterly funny and amusing through constant repetition of laughter from a gadget that emits ('fake') humorous responses. Its purpose is to be a stimulus to the audience's enjoyment (and consumption) of entertainment, to enhance audience laughter. However, while the comic frame of slapstick clowning does not encourage an empathetic or psychologically nuanced connection with the protagonists of a show, thus allowing us to enjoy the distance between us and the (wicked) clown scenario through humor, the laugh track in *The Big Bang Theory* serves as both distancing *and* immersion, while tapping into the erosion of authenticity and post-human interaction and communication.

The laugh track—"a cornerstone of American television comedy" and "culturally encoded form of social algorithmics" (Nickl, 2024, pp. 160, 166)—is a technological replication of amusement behaviors that, externally induced, if not controlled, disconnects the audience and comedic content, "as the decision to laugh is no longer a personal one, but a preprogrammed response and a choice made by others" (Nickl, 2024, p. 163; Nickl explores the history of canned laughter, and the ways it is now being interpreted as marking "the onset of a culture of mediated manipulation" (p. 161)). The laugh track is seen as coercive or 'contagious'—it encourages us to laugh, even at situations that we would not normally find amusing (Brewer, 2018, p. 12; Pradhan et al., 2021). So how does the reception of the experience of science-related humor and women scientists change when there is a technological mediation interface between the audience laughing and the laughter itself—when "[t]he laugh box, while augmenting the comedic experience by providing consistent and controlled laughter, also distances us from our natural, spontaneous reactions to humor" (Nickl, 2024, p. 163)? To what extent does canned laughter, which mimics the collective social laugh, influences our perception of the humor situations outlined above—for example, when Sheldon removes Amy from her project (S12E05)?

Given that, as we have seen in Chapter 1, comedy is a form of social commentary (at least in the Western context) and that canned laughter, which artificially induces positive emotions, embodies a detachment from the recognition and response to humor (and thus human agency), the risk of reducing comedy to eliciting a conditioned response, "rather than a form of art that encourages critical thinking and social awareness" (Nickl, 2024, p. 163), has to be considered. The laugh track that is supposed to fuel our amusement is thus highly problematic, for example, when Amy, seriously distressed—but accompanied by canned laughter—reacts to the pressure of her work and of being a potential female Nobel prize candidate by saying "I am a failure, I can't do this" (S12E19). As Brewer indicates, being carried away by the laugh track can lead to inauthenticity and self-deception (or "bullshit taste"), a disconnection from our own humor preferences (Brewer, 2018, p. 17; on the laugh track in *The Big Bang Theory* see p. 13). To put it in dramatic terms: we can become laughter victims. While we see the risks of exaggeration and the benefits of a healthy critique of these ideas and ideologies (Brewer, 2018, p. 19), our reading of these phenomena suggests that there may be reasons to remain aware of this kind of animated laughter, deliberately deployed to fabricate social interactions around the mediated experience of female scientists, which also applies to the not so different, asynchronous enactment of human emotion and amusement in another of our selected comedy series: *Zoey's Extraordinary Playlist*.

THE ABSURDIST COMIC FRAME
AND THE WOMAN SCIENTIST

Zoey, the woman engineer in *Zoey's Extraordinary Playlist* experiences moments of surprise when her surroundings explode into danced musical routines in varying degrees of complexity; an alternative dimension that gives her insights into the thoughts of her work colleagues, which influences her own work experience as a programmer and group leader. In fact, the dancing and singing surprises her within the show (intradiegetically) and us, the audience external to the narrative (extradiegetically), with its rapidity, bizarreness and unexplained nature (especially in S01E01 and S01E02). While much of the dancing is 'Back to School'/*Grease*- or flashmob-like, the humor of the "maximally counterintuitive" (Foster & Keane, 2019, p. 84) dance explosions is particularly incongruous and (therefore) funny when it reveals colleagues' hidden professional desires, as when a male coder shares his megalomaniacal competitive professional ambitions in a gangsta-hip-hop-meets-crip-walk routine (see S01E01 around 29:00). This 'dramatic' performance and theatrical interlude communicates who the colleague 'really is' behind the social role he inhabits in his everyday life (a strategy commonly used in contemporary TV series, De Kosnik, 2010, p. 377).

Surprise on different levels in conjunction with the disparity between Zoey's 'real' world and the song and dance injections thus generates the show's absurdist humor (Couder, 2019, p. 2). Unexplainable, with no possible resolution (especially in the show's first two episodes), the out-of-the-blue dancing and singing acts as a distancing effect—an absurdist comic frame. "Absurdist humor", Couder explains, "reveals a world that is familiar and yet at the same time unfamiliar [...] it is caused by an incongruity that defies the expectation of (logical) causality" (Couder, 2019, p. 13). The incongruity, a tension between presence and absence of meaning, is situated at the content level within the show but also owes its existence to the way we, the audience, engage with the interplay between familiarity and unfamiliarity. We laugh at it—the "breakdown of logic" and "absence or refusal of meaning" (Noonan, 2014, p. 1)—which leans toward nonsense. All of this becomes particularly interesting when Zoey herself has involuntary bouts of dancing, as at the beginning of S01E02. Although a dream (or, rather, a comic nightmare?), this opening not only recalls the famous "Day-o!" scene in the 1988 comedy film *Beetlejuice*, in which a supernatural clown possesses the protagonists and makes them dance ("Day-o! Banana Boat Song")—a clearly comic intertext—but this also casts a distancing shadow over the woman scientist. Unfathomable and absurd, the woman scientist's bodily expressions do not encourage any empathetic or psychologically nuanced connection with her as this humor simply does not make sense; it fails to achieve causal elaboration (Foster & Keane, 2019). We laugh at, not with, her, the absurdist scientist, given that the more "excessive the behavior of the characters the more likely we are to read it as unrealistic and absurd" (Peacock, 2014, p. 36). Repeating the surprise-based laugh-inducing pattern of the first episode, which stimulates specific, intentional and predictable mood changes in the audience (see Nickl, 2024, p. 172), the function of Zoey's involuntarily absurdist dancing in Episode 2 is not so different from canned laughter: by exploiting the power of surprise and incongruity through bodily movement, "laughter can be fed to us upon command, instructed from afar" (Nickl, 2024, p. 175). Thus, whether through absurd dancing or laughter from a machine, it is not only the development and interaction of the scientists that influences our perception of them in a rather ambiguous way, but also their framing through comedic devices—comic frames—which, in both *The Big Bang Theory* and *Zoey's Extraordinary Playlist*, render them and influence our own engagement with their humorous moments and situations. And this is also true of the comedy-drama TV series *Never Have I Ever*.

CULTURAL CRITIQUE THROUGH THE COMIC FRAME AND THE WOMAN SCIENTIST

Although not sitcoms per se (unlike *The Big Bang Theory*), *Never Have I Ever* and *Zoey's Extraordinary Playlist* deal with stock social situations, especially revolving around more or less (un)believable romantic interests; they are clearly not serious shows, and can be described as "diverting amusement" (Mills, 2009, pp. 1, 2). Both series, *Never Have I Ever* and *Zoey's Extraordinary Playlist*, epitomize what Abigail de Kosnik has called "television's turn to theatricality" (2010), including their treatment of science themes. Their woman scientist protagonists "consciously make spectacles of themselves in the eyes of others, and by exposing themselves in this way, they realize and reveal core truths about themselves" (De Kosnik, 2010, p. 370). While Zoey is certainly a spectacle in her own right, as we have seen above, the scientist Kamala in *Never Have I Ever* is surrounded by the 'spectacle' of her family and her male scientist colleagues (see, e.g., S02E01 and S02E04). Although at the content and interaction level of the show, she is framed in terms of humor—particularly sexist humor (see above)—by her male science colleagues, we argue that, unlike in *The Big Bang Theory* and *Zoey's Extraordinary Playlist*, the comic frame *around* her interactions with those male scientists does not only mock *them*, but also acts as a form of cultural critique.

Clumsy and unattractive, Evan Safstrom, the head research assistant of Kamala's lab at CalTech—who calls himself the 'hero' of his group and sloppily and irresponsibly destroys lab equipment as well as (her) samples while imitating a scene from *The Matrix*—shows as much a lack of elasticity and absent-mindedness as another character of the show, Mr. Shapiro (a high school teacher), which is interpreted as a comic frame by Reddi and Richards (referring to philosopher Henri Bergson's ideas on the nature of comedy, 2024, p. 91). In Shapiro's case this comic frame is used to mock and challenge (American) Whiteness, but similar to Shapiro's comedic existence in the show, Safstrom "is a reminder of the normative assumptions" (Reddi & Richards, 2024, 92) we make about scientists' identity, what it means to be a scientist, and who gets to be a scientist, which, equally, raises questions about citizenship—science citizenship (Schibeci & Lee, 2003). That is to say, he explicitly conforms to the straight, white, male, and socially awkward stereotype of the scientist. From this perspective, the comic frame unfolding around the male lab scientists in *Never Have I Ever* provides a stage for comedic critiques of the supposedly male 'right to science citizenship'.

As our excursion into comic frames has shown, when we zoom out from the woman scientist, her occupation with science and her direct interaction with the male entourage (analyzed in detail above), we discover the power of the comic frame in situating humor as a social corrective (Kuipers, 2011, p. 71) and antihistamine, alleviating the symptoms of chauvinistic science rivalry, but also in shaping our own (the audience's) experience of science-oriented humor. The source of science-related humor, and humor reaction, is thus impressively diverse, and potentially deceptive, in TV comedies, especially sitcoms, "where technique is not needed at all because the sound engineer will add hysterical laughter of the imaginary audience in the right moments so the real audience knows when to laugh..." (Droznin, 2016, p. 149). And we can laugh in a range of ways at—and with—comic scientists. Some of these ways are engineered to make us feel good, they "encourage the television viewing audience to laugh at the jokes" (Brewer, 2018, p. 18) or "to trick others into believing that we do [appreciate the joke]" (Nickl, 2024, p. 165), which challenges the integrity of our laughter. As Ben Nickl highlights, "[m]ediation technologies have trained us to crave these expressions, creating a cycle of consumption that continually feeds our desire for this enhanced, mediated reality" (2024, p. 173). The woman scientist's reality as depicted in TV comedies is thus also mediated *by* laughter, which brings to mind Charney and Schwartz's (1995, p. 8) ideas on the role of film in society more broadly, pointing to the fact that the zone between representation and reality has been called an "epistemological twilight"—"a striking phrase that captures the ambiguity of the interaction between a reality that can be grasped only in its representations and the representations that feed off and form part of that ongoing reality". This blurred boundary between what is real and what is represented underscores the importance of interrogating the stories we tell about women in STEM, and whether they are the stories we deserve.

A Final Note on Women Scientists in the Broader Universe of The Big Bang Theory

Although *The Big Bang Theory* remains one of the most commercially successful TV shows depicting women scientists, with media commentary still being published at time of this book's publication six years after the show ended in 2019 (see Crabtree, 2024, The Feed, 2024), there is less discussion of the spin-off prequel to *The Big Bang Theory*—*Young Sheldon* (2017–2024) and its comedic representations of STEM. Unlike *The Big Bang Theory*, *Young Sheldon* depicts very few women scientists, however, the few humorous elements in their depictions are based in gendered stereotypes. One episode shows a woman scientist doing a university research study on intelligence in twins, which Sheldon and his twin sister, Missy, take part in (*A Research Study and Czechoslovakian Wedding Pastries*, S02E5). The humorous elements in scenes related to the woman scientist involved, for example: Missy encouraging her to change the way she dresses, and to wear her hair down to enhance her appearance; and discussing Missy's belief that one of the male scientists has a crush on the woman scientist (*A Research Study and Czechoslovakian Wedding Pastries*, S02E5). In later scenes the woman scientist is depicted following Missy's advice and altering her appearance and asking the male scientist on a date (*A Research Study and Czechoslovakian Wedding Pastries*, S02E5). Although a light-hearted scene, the only humor related to the women scientist is based in stereotypes of beauty, femininity and relationships, ultimately making her appear less professional than her male colleague. This lack of named women in STEM characters fitting our inclusion criteria (see Chapter 3) caused us to exclude *Young Sheldon* from the present study. But we include these remarks to highlight that even in more recent years, shows set in STEM environments can fail to pass a Bechdel-Wallace test of who is portrayed in the TV laboratory, despite some gains in the field.

References

Abel, M. (2024). Do workers discriminate against female bosses? *Journal of Human Resources, 59*(2), 470–501. https://doi.org/10.3368/jhr.1120-113 18R3

Acuff, D. S., & Reiher, R. H. (1997). *What kids buy and why.* Free Press.

Ahlqvist, S., London, B., & Rosenthal, L. (2013). Unstable identity compatibility: How gender rejection sensitivity undermines the success of women in science, technology, engineering, and mathematics fields. *Psychological Science, 24*(9), 1644–1652. https://doi.org/10.1177/0956797613476048

Banchefsky, S., Westfall, J., Park, B., & Judd, C. (2016). But you don't look like a scientist!: Women scientists with feminine appearance are deemed less likely to be scientists. *Sex Roles, 75*(3–4), 95–109. https://doi.org/10.1007/s11 199-016-0586-1

Barreca, R. (1991). *They used to call me snow white. . . But i drifted: women's strategic use of humor.* Viking Penguin.

Bell, S., Yates, L., May, R., & Nguyen, H. (2015). Women in the science research workforce: Identifying and sustaining the diversity advantage. *University of Melbourne, LH Martin Institute.* Retrieved from https://www. raci.org.au/common/Uploaded%20files/Website%20files/About%20pages/ Policies/women%20in%20science.pdf

Benwell, B. (2007). New sexism? *Journalism Studies, 8*(4), 539–549. https:// doi.org/10.1080/14616700701411797

Brewer, K. L. (2018). Don't make me laugh! Morality, ethics, and the laugh track. *Studies in American Humor, 4*(1), 10–36. https://doi.org/10.5325/ studamerhumor.4.1.0010

Britton, D. M. (2017). Beyond the chilly climate: The salience of gender in women's academic careers. *Gender and Society, 31*(1), 5–27. https://doi.org/ 10.1177/0891243216681494

Brodzinsky, D. M., Barnet, K., & Aiello, J. R. (1981). Sex of subject and gender identity as factors in humor appreciation. *Sex Roles, 7*, 561–573.

Buijzen, M., & Valkenburg, P. M. (2004). Developing a typology of humor in audiovisual media. *Media Psychology, 6*(2), 147–167. https://doi.org/10.1207/s1532785xmep0602_2

Burton, T. (Director). (1988). Day-o! Banana boat song scene [Film clip]. In *Beetlejuice*. YouTube. https://www.youtube.com/watch?v=PBpn0U9dFYE. Accessed 17 August 2024.

Charney, L., & Schwartz, V. R. (1995). *Cinema and the invention of modern life*. University of California Press.

Cole, K. K. (2015). "It's like she's eager to be verbally abused": Twitter, trolls, and (en)gendering disciplinary rhetoric. *Feminist Media Studies, 15*(2), 356–358. https://doi.org/10.1080/14680777.2015.1008750

Couder, O. (2019). Problem solved? Absurdist humour and incongruity-resolution. *Journal of Literary Semantics, 48*, 1–21. https://doi.org/10.1515/jls-2019-2005

Crabtree, E. (2024). The Big Bang Theory cast: Where are they now?—*US Magazine*. https://www.usmagazine.com/entertainment/pictures/the-big-bang-theory-cast-where-are-they-now/

Crawford, M. (2003). Gender and humor in social context. *Journal of Pragmatics, 35*(9), 1413–1430. https://doi.org/10.1016/S0378-2166(02)00183-2

Dasgupta, N., & Stout, J. G. (2014). Girls and women in science, technology, engineering, and mathematics. *Policy Insights from the Behavioral and Brain Sciences, 1*(1), 21–29. https://doi.org/10.1177/2372732214549471

De Kosnik, A. (2010). Drama is the cure for gossip: Television's turn to theatricality in a time of media transition. *Modern Drama, 53*(3), 370–389. https://doi.org/10.3138/md.53.3.370

Drakett, J., Rickett, B., Day, K., & Milnes, K. (2018). Old jokes, new media—Online sexism and constructions of gender in Internet memes. *Feminism & Psychology, 28*(1), 109–127. https://doi.org/10.1177/0959353517727560

Droznin, A. (2016). *Physical actor training: What shall I do with the body they gave me?* Taylor & Francis Group.

Eagly, A. H. (2007). Female leadership advantage and disadvantage: Resolving the contradictions. *Psychology of Women Quarterly, 31*(1), 1–12. https://doi.org/10.1111/j.1471-6402.2007.00326.x

Ellemers, N., Van den Heuvel, H., De Gilder, D., Maass, A., & Bonvini, A. (2004). The underrepresentation of women in science: Differential commitment or the queen bee syndrome? *British Journal of Social Psychology, 43*(3), 315–338. https://doi.org/10.1348/0144666042037999

Eren, E. (2022). Never the right time: Maternity planning alongside a science career in academia. *Journal of Gender Studies, 31*(1), 136–147. https://doi.org/10.1080/09589236.2020.1858765

Fairweather, N. (2019). *Media's role in public perceptions of STEM: Understanding television portrayals of scientists through examination of the Big Bang Theory* (Ph.D.). Regent University. In *ProQuest Dissertations and Theses.* http://www.proquest.com/docview/2219284971/abstract/7666B0 C0AE2E47F3PQ/1

Flicker, E. (2003). Between brains and breasts: Women scientists in fiction film: On the marginalization and sexualization of scientific competence. *Public Understanding of Science, 12*(3), 307–318. https://doi.org/10.1177/096 3662503123009

Flicker, E. (2008). Women scientists in mainstream film: Social role models— Contribution to the public understanding of science from the perspective of film sociology. In P. Weingart & B. Hüppauf (Eds.), *Science Images and Popular Images of the Sciences,* (pp. 241–256). Routledge.

Ford, T. E., Wentzel, E. R., & Lorion, J. (2001). Effects of exposure to sexist humor on perceptions of normative tolerance of sexism. *European Journal of Social Psychology, 31*(6), 677–691. https://doi.org/10.1002/ejsp.56

Ford, T. E., Woodzicka, J. A., Triplett, S. R., & Kochersberger, A. O. (2013). Sexist humor and beliefs that justify social sexism. *Current Research in Social Psychology, 21*(7), 64–81.

Ford, T. E., Teeter, S. R., Richardson, K., & Woodzicka, J. A. (2017). Putting the brakes on prejudice rebound effects: An ironic effect of disparagement humor. *The Journal of Social Psychology, 157*(4), 458–473. https://doi.org/ 10.1080/00224545.2016.1229254

Foster, M. I., & Keane, M. T. (2019). The role of surprise in learning: Different surprising outcomes affect memorability differentially. *Topics in Cognitive Science, 11*(1), 75–87. https://doi.org/10.1111/tops.12392

Francis, B., Archer, L., Moote, J., de Witt, J., & Yeomans, L. (2017). Femininity, science, and the denigration of the girly girl. *British Journal of Sociology of Education, 38*(8), 1097–1110. https://doi.org/10.1080/01425692.2016. 1253455

Franzini, L. R. (1996). Feminism and women's sense of humor. *Sex Roles, 11*(12), 811–819. https://doi.org/10.1007/BF01544094

Gheorghiu, A. I., Callan, M. J., & Skylark, W. J. (2017). Facial appearance affects science communication. *Proceedings of the National Academy of Sciences, 114*(23), 5970–5975. https://doi.org/10.1073/pnas.1620542114

Gill, R. (2007). Postfeminist media culture: Elements of a sensibility. *European Journal of Cultural Studies, 10*(2), 147–166. https://doi.org/10.1177/136 7549407075898

Greenwood, D., & Isbell, L. M. (2002). Ambivalent sexism and the dumb blonde: Men's and women's reactions to sexist jokes. *Psychology of Women Quarterly, 26*(4), 341–350. https://doi.org/10.1111/1471-6402.t01-2-00073

Haas, M., Koeszegi, S. T., & Zedlacher, E. (2016). Breaking patterns? How female scientists negotiate their token role in their life stories. *Gender, Work & Organization, 23*(4), 397–413. https://doi.org/10.1111/gwao.12124

Hall, R. M., & Sandler, B. R. (1982). *The classroom climate: A chilly one for women?* Project on the Status and Education of Women.

Herman, C. (2009). Paying the price: The impact of maternity on career progression of women scientists and engineers in Europe. In S. Beiträge von Ihsen, J. Klumpers, S. Pageler, R. Ulrich, & B. Wieneke-Toutaoui (Eds.), *Gender and Diversity in Engineering and Science,* (pp. 47–56). The Association of German Engineers.

Hessler, D. (2020). Whose pain is it, anyway? On avatar embodiment, slapstick performances, and virtual pain. *Comedy Studies, 11*(1), 85–103. https://doi.org/10.1080/2040610X.2019.1692550

Hewlett, S. A., Luce, C. B., Servon, L. J., Sherbin, L., Shiller, P., Sosnovich, E., & Sumberg, K. (2008). The Athena factor: Reversing the brain drain in science, engineering, and technology. *Harvard Business Review Research Report, 10094,* 1–100.

Johnson, A. M. (1992). Language ability and sex affect humor appreciation. *Perceptual and Motor Skills, 75*(2), 571–581. https://doi.org/10.2466/pms.1992.75.2.571

Jürgens, A.-S., Darragh, L., Peace, P., Agha, R., Viana, J. N. and Richards, I. (2024). Studying science in pop culture through textual analysis. An introduction to examining science in visual texts—Street art, comics and (animated) film. *Journal of Science Communication, 23*(03), Y01. https://doi.org/10.22323/2.23030401

Kirby, D. A. (2011). *Lab coats in Hollywood: Science, scientists, and cinema.* Cambridge: MIT Press. https://doi.org/10.7551/mitpress/8483.001.0001

Kuipers, G. (2011). The politics of humour in the public sphere: Cartoons, power, and modernity in the first transnational humour scandal. *European Journal of Cultural Studies, 14*(1), 63–80. https://doi.org/10.1177/1367549410370072

LaFollette, M. C. (1988). Eyes on the stars: Images of women scientists in popular magazines. *Science, Technology, & Human Values, 13*(3–4), 262–275. https://doi.org/10.1177/016224398801303-407

London, B., Downey, G., Romero-Canyas, R., Rattan, A., & Tyson, D. (2012). Gender-based rejection sensitivity and academic self-silencing in women. *Journal of Personality and Social Psychology, 102*(5), 961–979. https://doi.org/10.1037/a0026615

McIntosh, H. (2014). Representations of female scientists in the Big Bang Theory. *Journal of Popular Film and Television, 42*(4), 195–204. https://doi.org/10.1080/01956051.2014.896779

Medhurst, A. (2007). *A national joke: Popular comedy and English cultural identities*. Routledge.

Mills, B. (2009). *The sitcom*. Edinburgh University Press.

Mitchell, M., & McKinnon, M. (2019). 'Human' or 'objective' faces of science? Gender stereotypes and the representation of scientists in the media. *Public Understanding of Science, 28*(2), 177–190. https://doi.org/10.1177/096 3662518801257

Netchaeva, E., Kouchaki, M., & Sheppard, L. D. (2015). A man's (precarious) place: Men's experienced threat and self-assertive reactions to female superiors. *Personality and Social Psychology Bulletin, 41*(9), 1247–1259. https://doi.org/10.1177/0146167215593491

Nickl, B. (2024). Synthetic laughter: Technologies of humour mediation and the moral issues of the laugh box. In B. Nickl & M. Rolfe (Eds.), *Moral dimensions of humour: Essays on humans, heroes and monsters* (pp. 160–184). Tampere UP.

Noonan, W. (2014). Absurdist humor. In S. Attardo (Ed.), *Encyclopedia of Humor Studies*, (pp. 1–4). SAGE Reference.

Peacock, L. (2014). *Slapstick and comic performance: Comedy and pain*. Basingstoke: Palgrave Macmillan. https://doi.org/10.1057/978113743 8973

Peacock, L. (2020). Battles, blows and blood: Pleasure and terror in the performance of clown violence. *Comedy Studies, 11*(1), 74–84. https://doi.org/10.1080/2040610X.2019.1692549

Pradhan, S., Pradhan, S., Laraway, S., & Snycerski, S. (2021). "No laughing matter": The influence and necessity of the laugh track on humor and enjoyability in a comedic sitcom. *The Journal of Communication and Media Studies, 6*(4), 1–14. https://doi.org/10.18848/2470-9247/CGP/v06i04/1-14

Reddi, M., & Richards, J. (2024). Never have I ever... Challenged whiteness. In H. W. Holladay & C. L. Classen (Eds.), *Television sitcom and cultural crisis*, (pp. 85–97). Routledge.

Riquelme, A. R., Carretero-Dios, H., Megías, J. L., & Romero-Sánchez, M. (2023). Subversive humor against sexism: Conceptualization and first evidence on its empirical nature. *Current Psychology, 42*(19), 16208–16221. https://doi.org/10.1007/s12144-019-00331-9

Rosser, S.V. (2018). Breaking into the lab: Engineering progress for women in science and technology. *International Journal of Gender, Science and Technology, 10*(2), 213–232. https://genderandset.open.ac.uk/index.php/gender andset/article/view/490.

Rossiter, M. W. (1993). The Matilda effect in science. *Social Studies of Science, 23*(2), 325–341. https://doi.org/10.1177/030631293023002004

Schibeci, R., & Lee, L. (2003). Portrayals of science and scientists, and 'science for citizenship.' *Research in Science & Technological Education, 21*(2), 177–192.

Shachar, O. (2000). Spotlighting women scientists in the press: Tokenism in science journalism. *Public Understanding of Science, 9*(4), 347–358. https://doi.org/10.1088/0963-6625/9/4/301

Shifman, L., & Lemish, D. (2010). Between feminism and fun(ny)mism: Analysing gender in popular internet humour. *Information, Communication & Society, 13*(6), 870–891. https://doi.org/10.1080/13691180903490560

Soucy-Humphreys, J., Judd, K., & Jürgens, A.-S. (2023). *Challenging the stereotype through humor? Comic female scientists in animated TV series for young audiences. 7*(1024602). https://doi.org/10.3389/fcomm.2022.1024602

Steele, C. M. (1997). A threat in the air: How stereotypes shape intellectual identity and performance. *American Psychologist, 52*(6), 613–629. https://doi.org/10.1037/0003-066X.52.6.613

Steinke, J. (2005). Cultural representations of gender and science: Portrayals of female scientists and engineers in popular films. *Science Communication, 27*(1), 27–63. https://doi.org/10.1177/1075547005278610

Steinke, J. (2012). Portrayals of female scientists in the mass media. In A.N. Valdivia (Ed.) *The International Encyclopedia of Media Studies*. Wiley. https://doi.org/10.1002/9781444361506.wbiems070

The Feed. (2024). The Big Bang Theory reunion: When and where can you witness the comeback?. *The Economic Times*. https://economictimes.indiatimes.com/news/international/us/the-big-bang-theory-reunion-when-and-where-can-you-witness-the-comeback/articleshow/107601886.cms

Tuchman, G. (2000). The symbolic annihilation of women by the mass media. In L. Crothers & C. Lockhart (Eds.), *Culture and politics: A reader* (pp. 150–174). Palgrave Macmillan US. https://doi.org/10.1007/978-1-349-62397-6_9

Weitekamp, M. A. (2015). 'We're physicists': Gender, genre and the image of scientists in The Big Bang Theory. *The Journal of Popular Television, 3*(1), 75–92. https://doi.org/10.1386/jptv.3.1.75_1

Woodzicka, J. A., & Ford, T. E. (2010). A framework for thinking about the (not-so-funny) effects of sexist humor. *Europe's Journal of Psychology, 6*(3), Article 3. https://doi.org/10.5964/ejop.v6i3.217

Worth, A., Augoustinos, M., & Hastie, B. (2016). "Playing the gender card": Media representations of Julia Gillard's sexism and misogyny speech. *Feminism & Psychology, 26*(1), 52–72. https://doi.org/10.1177/0959353516055544

Yıldırım, B., Öcal, E., & Şahin-Topalcengiz, E. (2021). STEM in movies: female preservice teachers' perspectives on movie "Hidden Figures." *Journal of Baltic Science Education, 20*(5), 740–758. https://doi.org/10.33225/jbse/21.20.740

CHAPTER 6

"You Winning a Nobel Prize Would Be an Inspiration to All Women": Conclusion

Abstract This chapter of *Women Scientists in American Television Comedy: Beakers, Big Bangs and Broken Hearts* concludes this volume by highlighting the significant role humor in TV comedies plays in shaping public perceptions of women scientists and promoting STEM careers among young women. The analysis of 47 episodes from *Never Have I Ever, The Big Bang Theory* and *Zoey's Extraordinary Playlist* revealed that irony and satire were the most common humor types used. These forms of humor often criticized male characters and patriarchal structures, aligning with feminist humor that challenges traditional gender stereotypes and power dynamics. The chapter emphasizes that humor makes science relatable and enjoyable, potentially increasing engagement with scientific concepts. The study acknowledges its limitation to Western, specifically American, cultural contexts and suggests future research explore humorous portrayals of women scientists in non-Western media. It also calls for empirical studies to assess how TV comedies influence audience perceptions and behaviors regarding science. The findings demonstrate that humor in TV comedies can both reinforce and subvert gender stereotypes, using irony, satire and ridicule to challenge misogynistic attitudes and highlight the challenges faced by women scientists. Ultimately, the study underscores the importance of diverse and complex representations of women in STEM, showing that humor can be a powerful tool for social change and empowerment in science communication.

© The Author(s), under exclusive license to Springer Nature
Switzerland AG 2025
K. Judd et al., *Women Scientists in American Television Comedy*,
Palgrave Studies in Science and Popular Culture,
https://doi.org/10.1007/978-3-031-81525-6_6

Keywords Humor and STEM careers · Diverse representation · Humor for social change · Humor and science communication

Women Scientists in American Television Comedy: Beakers, Big Bangs and Broken Hearts has shown that the representation of women scientists can have powerful cultural impacts. As Sheldon remarks to Amy: "You winning a Nobel Prize would be an inspiration to all women" (*The Big Bang Theory S12E19*)—not just in the universe of the show, but for many viewers too. This concluding chapter emphasizes the crucial need for varied and nuanced portrayals of women in STEM, demonstrating that humor and popular culture can serve as potent instruments in science communication for social change and empowerment.

Science and entertainment are "two of the most powerful cultural institutions that humans have developed to understand and explore their world" (Kirby, 2017, p. 291). Creating an immersive "melding of attention, imagery and feelings" (Davies et al., 2019, p. 8), humor-based narrative and visual fiction can influence audiences' perceptions of their own worlds (Mathies, 2020; Stroud, 2008) and provide enjoyment. Enjoyment of culture, in the form of experiential encounters or consumptions of science-related entertainment, has been recognized as a resource for understanding and advancing science communication and engagement (Roberts et al., 2022). In fact, enjoyment is "a highly desirable component of all science communication" that "may evoke positive feelings and attitudes that may lead to subsequent, deeper encounters with science" and thus contribute to a "healthy scientific culture within society" (Burns et al., 2003, p. 197). As Kirby (2011, p. 11) argues, the "construction of science, then, becomes a promotional strategy where 'realism' is highlighted as an entertainment value". Humor is instrumental in making science interesting, and makes the scientists in TV comedies more 'human' and relatable (see Li, 2016 on *The Big Bang Theory*, without analyzing the humor in detail). Humor, as a strategy for relatability and enjoyment, can shape how viewers—especially young female audiences—perceive and identify with people in the field. As explored in earlier chapters, diverse representations of women scientists hold immense power to influence and encourage the uptake of STEM careers by women, however, we have found there are very few examples in television comedies, especially outside of America. Future research should examine the extent to which this may affect whether and how audiences identify with characters. Previous research has shown that perceived relatability to people in STEM fields is fundamental in sparking women's interest in STEM subjects, ultimately contributing to greater diversity in STEM subjects (Cheryan & Plaut, 2010). We suspect there is a role for popular culture to play in better representing STEM as a place where people can find community of others with similar identities. A natural progression of this work is to conduct qualitative research with audience groups to understand how they take on the implicit and explicit messages about women and STEM from television shows like those in our study. We recommend future work to explore audiences'—especially of young, female and gender-diverse people—processes of meaning-making (see, for example, Davies et al., 2019) around television comedies that portray women scientists. In the present study, we used the humor typology developed by Buijzen and Valkenburg (2004) as the basis for our analysis, although future research may also find value in the framework proposed by Woodzicka and Ford (2010) on the *effects* of sexist humor—applying this in a science communication context could add new insight to the field.

It is important to recognize that our study was limited to the representation of women scientists in a Western—specifically American—cultural context. From our purposive internet-based research, we found very few examples of non-American examples of women scientists in TV comedy. However, there are examples of women scientists in other genres, for example, the Chinese drama series *Broker* (2021) and Korean science-fiction series *The Silent Sea* (2021). As humor is not confined to the bounds of the comedy genre, humorous elements in depictions of such scientist characters may provide further insight into the intersectionality between gender, STEM, culture and humor. Future research could also focus on humorous representations of women scientists in non-Western comedy forms such as film and theatrical performances, to compare the influence of cultural context on both the humor typology and the representation of women scientists in these media.

It was beyond the scope of the present study to investigate the gendered influence of the production teams behind each show in our sample. As an industry, television production has long been a "*man*-made" art form (Coyle, 1988, p. 58), while women are the object of that art (Wallenberg & Jansson, 2021). Although television writing rooms are becoming more diverse, there remains much room for improvement

(Think Tank for Inclusion and Equity & Geena Davis Institute, 2022). Previous research has suggested some relationship between who makes television and who those shows depict (Linke & Prommer, 2021), but no research to date looks at this at the nexus of science and humor. This presents a research opportunity for exploration of how the intersectional makeup of teams behind the camera influence how the people and places of STEM are portrayed on the screen.

Qualitative research with smaller data collections has been criticized for not being transferrable to other settings (Quieros et al., 2017) and even for "yielding less societal use-value" because "there is no way of telling what is true and what is false" (Frykholm, 2021, p. 255). Although this could be seen as a limitation of this study, it is not the point of our research to say what is 'true' and what is 'false', not least because generalizing qualitative research is not the goal or interest of qualitative textual analysis (Gheondea-Eladi, 2014), the method we used. Our study explores intersections between (the cultural stream of) Science Communication, Humor Studies and Pop Culture/Popular Entertainment Studies—and thus spheres that tap into qualitative Humanities research, which uses approaches and modes of criticism that are interpretive, critical or speculative in nature. Within this context, we explored *meaning production* and how it can be studied as a process that is contextualized and inextricably linked to broader social and cultural practices (Jensen, 1991, p. 4). Given that pop culture is where collective understandings of science and scientists are created, and that pop cultural products exploring science themes are considered a form of "public pedagogy" (Giroux, 2010, p. 2), we were interested in discovering "deeper themes" in our material—and thus became "message investigator[s]" (De Castilla, 2017, p. 137; Jürgens et al., 2024). Feminist *reading methodologies* (beyond textual analysis), enacting feminist theorization, can deliver a more nuanced understanding and interpretation of the structural inequality in these contexts in the future (see, e.g., Cox, 2022). Future empirical studies should focus on audience influence and how TV comedies can affect perceptions of (behavioral) norms and changes can take our discoveries on the cultural ideas and images of scientist characters to 'test' how exactly enjoyment and different humor responses in relation to the scientist at stake can shape, reframe or confirm science-related opinions (cf. Burns et al., 2003, p. 190). Research has shown that narrative and visual fiction fostering identification can influence audiences' perceptions of their own worlds (Mathies, 2020; Stroud, 2008), and it would be fascinating to explore in future studies how exactly this manifests in the context of comedic women scientists in TV comedies. This would be worth exploring, as research has shown that eliciting emotional responses (such as amusement and enjoyment) in audiences can increase engagement with scientific concepts and perceptions of their usefulness or meaningfulness (Bilandzic et al., 2020; Joubert et al., 2019).

Overall, in this study we analyzed the relationship between "what is shown and what can be perceived as real" in selected episodes of science-related TV shows as sites of "cultural circulation"—where diverse discourses, aesthetic practices and the worlds of imagined scientists interact (Flicker, 2008, p. 243) and where stereotypes reveal the importance of cultural contexts for STEM fields. Informed by previous research on women stereotypes, humor theories and the cultural stream of Science Communication, we examined a total of 47 episodes of three popular TV comedies through textual analysis to better understand how their women scientist protagonists were portrayed through humor. We also reflected on how characters' portrayal reinforced or challenged gender conventions in these fictional representations of the scientific profession and (the reality of) science, and importantly, how humor drove these ideas in each show. Affirming the "increasingly prevalent sense that science communication is not external to (popular) culture" (Davies et al., 2019, p. 2), our study found that a wide range of humor types were used in the portrayal of different aspects of women scientists' life experiences. The most common types of humor were irony and satire, with much of the humor based on an awareness of existing gender stereotypes. The humorous use of irony often hides anti-feminist discourse through the use of ironic sexism. However, in line with feminist approaches to and understandings of humor, ironic humor was also frequently used to ridicule male characters and criticize patriarchal structures in STEM arenas. The results show both the versatility of humor and its power to reflect, reinforce and go beyond traditional gender stereotypes.

Humor in its various forms is known for its ability to harness creativity for new ways of knowing, "to interrupt the social reproduction of taken-for-granted knowledge" and to challenge the status quo (Longo, 2010, p. 118). Marginalized groups can use humor strategically to challenge powerlessness, while subversive humor—including satire or parody—leading to the creation of alternative scripts "within the parameters of the prevailing social order, ultimately to critique it", has been called "a form of micro-revolution" (Longo, 2010, p. 123). Perhaps not surprisingly, from a feminist perspective, humor can challenge the dominant ideological discourse (e.g. by showcasing its absurdities, Gillooly, 1991, p. 478). Feminist humor, which is specifically humor that challenges traditional views of gender and dominant constructions of femininity (Bing, 2004; Crawford, 2003; Riquelme et al., 2021), can serve as a vehicle to question well-established stereotypes and expose gendered power structures (Shifman & Lemish, 2010). As seen in our findings, contemporary TV comedies have employed this subversive humor form to challenge patriarchal structures in STEM, through the use of satire, irony and ridicule. In conjunction with complex women scientists representation that moves beyond the characteristics identified by Flicker (2008), feminist humor in TV comedies is a powerful tool to reform preconceptions of STEM, and empower young women to pursue STEM.

Like that of Buijzen and Valkenburg's (2004) humor typology, our study demonstrated that the use of humor differs slightly across different themes relating to the lived experience of the fictional woman scientist in television comedy. All TV shows feature humor and humorous devices to portray and communicate themes related to the experience of the woman scientist. In the representation of their expertise and competence, there were two dominant ways in which humor was used: first, through the use of humor in relation to explicit engagement with STEM, and second, through the use of ironic and satirical humor when contrasting the woman scientist to another character. Humor also served a purpose in highlighting the challenges of working with male colleagues, while also ridiculing the misogynistic attitudes held in workplaces. The balancing of professional and personal life as a woman scientist was also saliently addressed through humor, specifically using schadenfreude and ironic humor to emphasize misfortunes and failures in maintaining this balance. Common to most representations of the woman scientist is the use of irony and satire, which were used to communicate both anti-feminist and feminist discourses in the television programs. Anti-feminist discourses were often covert (e.g. ironic sexism), perpetuating misogynistic attitudes with little consequences due to the ironic nature of the disparagement humor. Exploring these different facets of humor in relation to women scientist protagonists our study clarifies and adds new dimensions to Petra Pansegrau's (2008, p. 257) statement that "[t]he media does not simply translate scientific information but are participants as well as producers of a dialogue about knowledge and have an important function within the public discourse". TV comedies, our study shows, play a crucial role in this process by contributing "to science's construction of meaning" (Flicker, 2008, p. 242).

Finally, and with a friendly wink to the fact that "[s]cience facts, without social significance are essentially meaningless and useless to society" (Burns et al., 2003, p. 196), our analysis elucidates how science is approached through humor in culture, showing that far from being the target of jokes in popular entertainment, science is a driver of performance style and contributes to the creation of comic forms. Within this context, comic representations of women scientists participate in and contribute to complex cultural inquiry and transmedial public discourses—and, ultimately, the cultural power and cultural work of science.

References

Bilandzic, H., Kinnebrock, S., & Klingler, M. (2020). The emotional effects of science narratives: A theoretical framework. *Media and Communication, 8*(1), 151–163. https://doi.org/10.17645/mac.v8i1.2602

Bing, J. M. (2004). Is feminist humor an oxymoron? *Women and Language, 27*(1), 22–33.

Buijzen, M., & Valkenburg, P. M. (2004). Developing a typology of humor in audiovisual media. *Media Psychology, 6*(2), 147–167. https://doi.org/10.1207/s1532785xmep0602_2

Burns, T. W., O'Connor, D. J., & Stocklmayer, S. M. (2003). Science communication: A contemporary definition. *Public Understanding of Science, 12*, 183–202. https://doi.org/10.1177/09636625030122004

Cheryan, S., & Plaut, V. C. (2010). Explaining underrepresentation: A theory of precluded interest. *Sex Roles, 63*(7–8), 475–488. https://doi.org/10.1007/s11199-010-9835-x

Cox, S. (Ed.). (2022). *Intersectional feminist readings of comics: Interpreting gender in graphic narratives.* Routledge.

Coyle, A. (1988). Behind the scenes: Women in television. In A. Coyle, & J. Skinner (Eds.), *Women and Work. Women in Society.* Palgrave Macmillan. https://doi.org/10.1007/978-1-349-19506-0_4

Crawford, M. (2003). Gender and humor in social context. *Journal of Pragmatics, 35*(9), 1413–1430. https://doi.org/10.1016/S0378-2166(02)00183-2

Davies, S. R., Halpern, M., Horst, M., Kirby, D. A., & Lewenstein, B. (2019). Science stories as culture: Experience, identity, narrative and emotion in public communication of science. *Journal of Science Communication, 18*(5).

De Castilla, C. R. (2017). Close reading. In M. Allen (Ed.), *The SAGE Encyclopedia of Communication Research Methods*, (pp. 138–139). SAGE. https://doi.org/10.4135/9781483381411.n58

Flicker, E. (2008). Women scientists in mainstream film: Social role models—Contribution to the public understanding of science from the perspective of film sociology. In P. Weingart & B. Hüppauf (Eds.), *Science Images and Popular Images of the Sciences*, (pp. 241–256). Routledge.

Frykholm, J. (2021). Critical thinking and the humanities: A case study of conceptualizations and teaching practices at the Section for Cinema Studies at Stockholm University. *Arts and Humanities in Higher Education, 20*(3), 253–273. https://doi.org/10.1177/1474022220948798

Gheondea-Eladi, A. (2014). Is qualitative research generalisable? *Journal of Community Positive Practices, 14*(2), 114–124. http://www.proquest.com/docview/1703229708/abstract/F11645E904C54AA5PQ/1.

Gillooly, E. (1991). Women and humor. *Feminist Studies, 17*, 473–491.

Giroux, H. A. (2010). *The mouse that roared: Disney and the end of innocence.* Rowman & Littlefield.

Jensen, P. (1991). Introduction: A qualitative turn. In N. W. Jankowski, & K. B Jensen (Eds.), *A Handbook of Qualitative Methodologies for Mass Sommunication Research*, (pp. 4). https://doi.org/10.4324/9780203409800.

Joubert, M., Davis, L., & Metcalfe, J. (2019). Storytelling: the soul of science communication. *Journal of Science Communication, 18*(05), E. https://doi.org/10.22323/2.18050501

Jürgens, A.-S., Darragh, L., Peace, P., Agha, R., Viana, J. N. & Richards, I. (2024). Studying science in pop culture through textual analysis. An introduction to examining science in visual texts — Street art, comics and (animated) film. *Journal of Science Communication, 23*(03), Y01. https://doi.org/10.22323/2.23030401

Kirby, D. A. (2011). *Lab coats in Hollywood: Science, scientists, and cinema.* MIT Press. https://doi.org/10.7551/mitpress/8483.001.0001

Kirby, D. A. (2017). The changing popular images of science. In K. H. Jamieson, D. M. Kahan, & D. A. Scheufele (Eds.), *The Oxford Handbook of the Science of Science Communication*, (pp 291–298). Oxford Handbooks Online. https://doi.org/10.1093/oxfordhb/9780190497620.013.32

Li, P. R. (2016). *Communicating science through entertainment television: How the sitcom The Big Bang Theory influences audience perceptions of science and scientists* [PhD Thesis]. The Australian National University. https://doi.org/10.25911/5d78d671bc21c

Linke, C., & Prommer, E. (2021). From fade-out into spotlight: An audiovisual character analysis (ACIS) on the diversity of media representation and production culture. *s*(1), 145–161. https://doi.org/10.24434/j.scoms.2021.01.010

Longo, M. (2010). Humour use and knowledge-making at the margins. *Canadian Social Work Review, 27*(1), 113–126.

Mathies, S. (2020). The simulated self—fiction reading and narrative identity. *Philosophia, 48*(1), 325–345. https://doi.org/10.1007/s11406-019-00079-3

Pansegrau, P. (2008). Stereotypes and images of scientists in fiction films. In P. Weingart & B. Hüppauf (Eds.), *Science Images and Popular Images of Science,* (pp. 33–51). Routledge. https://doi.org/10.4324/9780203939154-17

Quieros, A., Faria, D., & Almeida, F. (2017). Strengths and limitations of qualitative and quantitative research methods. *European Journal of Education Studies, 3*(9), 369–387. https://doi.org/10.5281/zenodo.88708

Riquelme, A. R., Carretero-Dios, H., Megías, J. L., & Romero-Sánchez, M. (2021). Joking for gender equality: Subversive humor against sexism motivates collective action in men and women with weaker feminist identity. *Sex Roles, 84*(1), 1–13. https://doi.org/10.1007/s11199-020-01154-w

Roberts, J., Milne, R., Middleton, A., Patch, C., & Morley, K. (2022). Opportunities for poaching: using the public's enjoyment of popular culture to foster dialogues around genetics. *Journal of Science Communication, 21*(06), Y01. https://doi.org/10.22323/2.21060401

Shifman, L., & Lemish, D. (2010). Between feminism and fun(ny)mism: Analysing gender in popular internet humour. *Information, Communication & Society, 13*(6), 870–891. https://doi.org/10.1080/13691180903490560

Stroud, S. R. (2008). Simulation, subjective knowledge, and the cognitive value of literary narrative. *The Journal of Aesthetic Education, 42*(3), 19–41. http://www.jstor.org/stable/25160288

Think Tank for Inclusion and Equity & Geena Davis Institute. (2022). *Behind the scenes: The state of inclusion and equity in TV writing 2022.* https://geenadavisinstitute.org/research/behind-the-scenes-the-state-of-inclusion-and-equity-in-tv-writing-2022/

Wallenberg, L., & Jansson, M. (2021). On and off screen: Women's work in the screen industries. *Gender, Work & Organization, 28*(6), 1991–1996. https://doi.org/10.1111/gwao.12748

Woodzicka, J. A., & Ford, T. E. (2010). A framework for thinking about the (not-so-funny) effects of sexist humor. *Europe's Journal of Psychology, 6*(3), Article 3. https://doi.org/10.5964/ejop.v6i3.217

INDEX

The manufacturer's authorised representative in the EU is Springer
Nature Customer Service Centre GmbH, Europaplatz 3, 69115 Heidelberg,
Germany. If you have any concerns regarding our products, please
contact ProductSafety@springernature.com

Printed and bound by CPI Group (UK) Ltd, Croydon, CR0 4YY
24/04/2026
02096371-0001